AF520136

# Requirement Validation: An Introduction

**Author**

Dr. Dhirendra Pandey

**Published By**

BONFRING™
Intellectual Integrity

**Requirement Validation: An Introduction**

Copyright © 2014 by Bonfring

All rights reserved. Authorized reprint of the edition published by Bonfring. No part of this book may be reproduced in any form without the written permission of the publisher.

Limits of Liability/Disclaimer of Warranty: The authors are solely responsible for the contents of the paper in this volume. The publishers or editors do not take any responsibility for the same in any manner. Errors, if any, are purely unintentional and readers are required to communicate such errors to the editors or publishers to avoid discrepancies in future. No warranty may be created or extended by sales or promotional materials. The advice and strategies contained herein may not be suitable for every situation. This work is sold with the understanding that the publisher is not engaged in rendering legal, accounting, or other professional services. If professional assistance is required, the services of a competent professional person should be sought. Further, reader should be aware that internet website listed in this work may have changed or disappeared between when this was written and when it is read.

Bonfring also publishes its books in a variety of electronic formats. Some content that appears in print may not be available in electronic books.

₹ 499

9 789383 459377 >

**ISBN 978-93-83459-37-7**

**Author**

**Dr. Dhirendra Pandey**

Assistant Professor, Department of Information Technology

Babasaheb Bhimrao Ambedkar University, Lucknow- India

**Published by**

**Bonfring**
292/2, 5th Street Extension, Gandhipuram,
Coimbatore-641 012. Tamilnadu, India.
E-mail: info@bonfring.org
Website: www.bonfring.org
Contact: 0422 3928700

## About the Author

**Dr. Dhirendra Pandey** has received his PhD (Computer Science) Degree from Devi Ahilya University, Indore (MP) - India and MPhil (Computer Science) Degree from Madurai Kamraj University, Madurai (TN) - India. Dr. Pandey has Graduate Degree and Master Degree in Computer Science from Guru Ghasidas University, Bilaspur, CG- India. Presently he is working in Babasaheb Bhimaro Ambedkar University, Lucknow as an Assistant Professor in the Department of Information Technology. He has published more than 40 international Journal and research article. Dr. Pandey has more than 09 Years of Teaching Experience and more than 08 years of research experiences. Dr. Dhirendra has guided more than 05 research students and more than 100 graduate students under his supervision.

# ACKNOWLEDGEMENT

First I thank God for having given me an opportunity and strength to complete this book successfully.

The writing of this Book has been an incredible journey and a monumental milestone in my academic life. I could not have embarked on this expedition and travelled this far without the passionate and continued support of supervisors, colleagues, friends, and family

I feel deep sense of gratitude for my father and mother who formed a base of my vision and taught me the good things that really matters in my life. I am also grateful to my elder brothers and sisters, who made my life, enlightened and made me to stand in this position. I couldn't have done it without them. In addition, my special thanks go to **Ms. Vandana Dubey**, my wife, for giving me ethical support during my study. Finally, I am grateful to my friends and colleagues who had made me comfortable, refreshing and joyful during my entire span of study.

I would like to express my gratitude to all those who gave me the possibility to complete this book especially Mohd. Waris Khan for providing help during writing of this Book

**Dr. Dhirendra Pandey**

# PREFACE

Requirement validation is an important aspects of requirement engineering which assists system analyst to make sure the requirement are unambiguous, complete and consistent, it is used in determining the correct requirement while verification determines that implementation is accurate with respect to user's need. The main objective of requirement validation framework is to clarify that requirement specification document is the acceptable description of the system which is going to be installed. The requirement validation framework incorporates various requirement validation techniques, which plays pilot role to identify the assume defects in the user's requirement. Requirement validation techniques can help in the completion of project within given schedule, cost, and budget according to the desired functionality. The requirement validation framework can be implementing in software projects, where the requirement plays an important role in designing of quality software development. In this kind of software project the user's requirement can be changed frequently over the software development periods. Therefore, it is necessary to check the consistency of SRS document because the SRS is the foundation of software design and development and the error assured in this phase may lead the problem in the later stage of the software development. Such as scheduling error, budget error and cost error. This book explore the various requirement validation techniques their aspects, approach and practices which are practiced in the software industry.

# CHAPTER 1

# REQUIREMENT ENGINEERING CONCEPTS

## 1.1. INTRODUCTION

The success of software development depends on the needs of its stakeholders and business environment. The identification and extraction of software requirements in effective manner is a key issue for project success. Generally, the cost of correcting a fault after implementing the system is an order of magnitude much higher than the cost of correcting a similar error during the requirement engineering phase [1]. Since requirement can change during development, it is important to manage the varying requirements [2]. The acceptance of requirement engineering process in software development is depends on social, technological and economical issues [3, 4, 5].

An important issue in Requirement Engineering (RE) is to conduct interview for requirements gathering in a systematic manner to avoid project failures. The capturing system requirement without using proper technique is the major factor in the failure of large software projects. In addition, poor requirements management can also be attributed in software projects failures [6]. The research indicates that failed or an abandoned system by aforesaid reasons causes the major loss in software industries. Thus, this research concentrates on the requirement gathering and interpreting problems between users and software developers, which is a necessary part of requirement engineering. It has been observed that the interviews between software developer and users are considered to be best practice in terms of methods for gathering user requirements as part of software development projects [7, 8]. The process of conducting successful conversations with users is the best exercise in requirement engineering.

The issue of effective participation between social and organizational elements plays an important role in requirement engineering [9]. One of the challenges is that each community interprets annotations in the light of their own background assumptions. This is especially problematic with non-interactive participation, where there is less opportunity to verify that the reader has interpreted requirements as it was intended. Thus, the participation difficulty between user and developers is the major problem in requirement engineering, which can affect the entire software development process. Requirements engineering phase of software development process is characterized by the strength and significance of participation activities. During this phase, various stakeholders will be able to communicate their requirements to the analysts. Similarly, the analysts will be able to communicate the specifications back to the stakeholders for their validation.

Nowadays, the security is a challenging issue to design and develop secure software. Also, it is observed that most of the software developers do not incorporate security mechanisms into Software Requirement Specification (SRS). For this reason, many of the potential clients are unable to supply their security related information to software developers, through which a schedule and security cost can reasonably be estimated. In addition, stakeholders are unaware about the security aspects, which is required for security or safety of the systems. Therefore, it is necessary to mention or includes the security and safety requirement into SRS documents [10]. The effectiveness of SRS document is also having quality impact on software development because upon which the software is to be developed.

The effectiveness of requirement engineering depends on its different issues and impact on software development process. The dimension of requirement engineering, requirement engineering tools and techniques, effectiveness of requirement engineering practices and recent requirement engineering practices are discussed in the following sub-sections. The dimensions of RE is discussed in Section 1.2. The RE tools and techniques are presented in Section 1.3. Section 1.4 describe recent RE practices. Various RE issues are presented in Section 1.5. The security and safety impact on requirement engineering is observed in Section1.6. Finally, Section 1.7 dictates the concluding remarks of the chapter.

## 1.2. DIMENSIONS OF RE

Requirements engineering phase is documented in the form of requirements specification. The requirements specification reflects the mutual understanding of the problem to be solved between the analyst and the client. The requirements specification serves as a starting point for the design phase. Several classifications have been proposed for requirements engineering. The requirement engineering is divided into three dimensions.

- Requirements elicitation
- Requirements Specification
- Requirements verification and validation

### 1.2.1. Requirements Elicitation

Requirements elicitation phase emphasizes on understanding the problems. It is observed that requirement analyst is not an expert in the domain being modeled. Through interaction with domain specialists, requirement analyst can build a sufficiently rich requirement model for the same domain.

Also, there are different disciplines involved in this process, which is too complicated. In many cases, the analyst is not only an outside observer of the domain to be modeled, simply eliciting facts from domain specialists. The term elicitation is used instead of capture, because the requirements are collected through work and investigation. The elicitation activities are closely related to the rest of the requirements engineering process.

There are several conventional techniques of elicitation such as, use of interviews, surveys and questionnaires to gather data from stakeholders. In addition, process models, organizational charts, standards and manuals can also used for requirement elicitation and development. Scenarios and use cases can be a very effective way to design concrete abstract descriptions into real-life examples, which helps in data gathering from stakeholders.

Observation or contextual techniques can also be a good way of eliciting the facts in contrast to stakeholders needs. It can be difficult for stakeholders to articulate fairly simple routines and tasks. Furthermore, the context and environment in which the stakeholder works can have great impact on requirement elicitation process. Group elicitation techniques such as, brainstorming, Joint Application Design (JAD) workshops are also valuable for requirement elicitation.

### 1.2.2. Requirements Specification

Once the problem is understood, it has to be described in the requirements specification document. The document describes the product to be delivered, regardless of development process. The requirements document or software requirements specification describes external behaviour of a software system [1, 2, 3]. The SRS is written by the developer in consultation with responsible users. A well written requirements document helps in meeting the desired goals of successful software within time limit. This document can also have adverse effect on the software if it is not written with good amount of care. Errors that are found in the requirements document are easy to fix, cost less and consume less time. If these documents are handled properly, errors can be reduced. Otherwise, fixing requirements errors during the design, coding or implementation phase can be a tedious task.

There are two types of errors that are found in requirements specification document; knowledge errors, and specification errors. The knowledge errors are caused due to inability to understand requirements whereas specification errors are caused due to lack of knowledge or experience of specifying requirements. A good requirements document has behavioural requirements and non-behavioural requirements. Behavioural requirements specify what the system does including its inputs and outputs. On the other hand, non-behavioural requirements include complete description of efficiency, reliability, security, portability and maintainability of requirement.

### 1.2.3. Requirements Verification and Validation

Once the requirement elicitation and specification are performed, the different parties involved in have to agree upon its nature. Further, the stakeholders have to ascertain that the correct requirements are stated (validation) and these requirements are stated in correct manner (verification). Requirement verification ensures that the subsequent products of the development process accurately reflect the requirements as it is documented [10, 15, 18]. Generally, developers do not perform verification process with care, whereas it may be mandatory throughout development. It has been observed that the automated support for verification and validation requires significant further research [18]. Now a day, verification becomes a matter of consistency management in which inconsistency is tolerated at certain points in development while at others consistency is checked and enforced. Therefore, the permissive view of verification presents a research challenge, which still has to be resolved [11, 21].

The validation of requirements engineering becomes necessary in the case, where these must be analyzed in order to establish the extent to which these are accurately embody the requirements [18, 23]. If there is a mismatch between the conception of stakeholders and requirements as these are documented then these might be ironed out. The research on validation concentrates on exploration and inspection of requirements. The verification tools, which allow multiple views and browsing of complex document and model structures, can be a significant research area in requirement verification [19, 20]. Researchers have also suggested that the research directions on specification assessment and annotation schemes for checking errors can be implemented into requirement verification tools [21, 22]. Generally, validation should be as tightly interleaved with requirements production as much as possible. In such cases, the requirement analyst may be faced with large amounts of information and analyst has no guidance about the processing and verification of information. Research on methods for providing such guidance is also a considerable challenge in requirement verification process.

### 1.3.RE TOOLS AND TECHNIQUES

The practical approaches for requirement engineering are also important for requirement gathering apart from theoretical concepts. Generally, a method, which is also referred to as methodology, provides a general approach. Whereas, a tool, usually but not always automated, provides a detailed step-by-step approach to carry out a method [5]. There are two main requirements engineering tools used to develop requirements, one is DOORS and another is RequisitePro [6].

RequisitePro is generally easy to use, able to import Word documents, and perform impact analysis using traceability matrices. RequisitePro also provides extremely flexible report generation capabilities since output may be directed to Word, Excel, raw text files, and formats supported by Visual Basic. However, such flexibilities require programming in Visual Basic. There are some limitations of RequisitePro. Its initial set-up must be well though-out and it does not link well with design tools such as, Rational Rose. However, RequisitePro tools can be used to link requirements to scenarios in Rational Rose. The RequisitePro is unable to help analyst in the analysis of requirements statements, although it only provide various requirement metrics such as, the number of changed requirements per unit of time. The analyst has to interpret the metrics in their own ways.

The primary benefit of DOORS is that it captures requirements and stores in a database management system. Hence, requirement traceability can be measured. But it is difficult to create documents in the formats that meet the needs of requirement engineers. Also, establishing traceability is a tedious process. Thus, requirement engineers need to set-up the initial document hierarchy because it is difficult to restructure it later (as with RequisitePro). Further, some of the researchers have already observed the allocation of requirements to multiple components within DOORS [8]. The result of this lack of knowledge on the part of requirement engineers is more than 25% of the requirements documents can be duplicate of one another [10]. Finally, the users complained that using Virtual PC to run DOORS on a MAC is slow in speed. Another researcher indicated that existing requirements tools are not so flexible enough to meet unanticipated needs, which are often occur. The analyst would like to have a repository with a predefined model of software artifacts as well as methods for defining new views of the repository contents. Both of which could be extended by analyst's team. Echoing the finding of a previous study, the team feels that the existing requirements engineering tools are unable to help analyst in requirement development [7].

In practice, there are two main effective requirement engineering technologies, i.e., Neural Impulse Actuator (NIA) and Mobile Technology Devices (MTD) [7, 8]. The NIA is a type of AI device that has the capability to read minds by incorporating an electromyogram, electro-encephalogram, and electrooculogram into a small headband and a little black box with a USB connector. it is a control system that can translate eye movements, facial muscle movements, and brain waves into game input. As a result, the NIA is a strange device that requires some unusual participation from the user. The NIA reads the brain waves, which indicates the thinking of stakeholders. On the user's PC, the NIA control software converts electrical potentials from the headband into usable input. This software separates the different frequencies in these potentials using proprietary algorithms instead of fast Fourier transforms. Running these algorithms on a continuously streaming flow of data can apparently control some serious CPU cycles. NIA can be used in the conjunction with other requirements engineering tools such as, interview, brainstorm and introspection in which the body gestures and mind reading is very much important to elicit the complete and accurate requirements. NIA technology is easily available and cheaper to buy.

The MTD provides automation to requirements elicitation and it is important for stakeholder communication regarding understanding and formulating the problems. The advance technology of mobile devices and mobile tools can significantly contribute to the automation of RE activities. Although other devices and tools used in different requirements gathering activities are mostly desktop computer or laptop base but because of their size and less mobility feature, they are usually not brought to the workplace of the stakeholders. Automating the requirements elicitation activities by using MTD can also be implemented into a web-based mobile RE tools [9].

### 1.4. Recent RE Practices

There are various requirement engineering practices such as, requirement elicitation, requirement analysis, requirement risk analysis, requirement specification, requirement verification, and requirement validation practices, which can help requirement engineers to define good requirements. These practices are discussed in the following Sub-sections with their properties and applications.

### 1.4.1. Elicitation Practices

Requirements elicitation is the process of identifying and consolidating various stakeholders' needs. A stakeholder is a person affected by a system, has an investment in it, or can affect its success. Typical stakeholders include customers, system analyst, regulators, software engineers, systems engineers, test engineers, and users. The stakeholders need is a business or operational problem that should be eliminated or an opportunity that should be exploited. There are following several important practices for eliciting the stakeholder's requirements such as, identify and involve stakeholders, identify the reason for developing a system, define a clear project vision with requirement glossary, identify user roles, and characteristics etc.

**Identifying and involving the stakeholders**

It is important to identify stakeholders because they have their own perspectives, agenda, priorities, drivers, and unique information concerning their environment, project feasibility, and solution strategies [9, 20]. By gathering and disseminating diverse information, all the stakeholders can share a common vision, from which they can set realistic expectations and develop high-quality requirements [3]. To develop high quality requirements, requirements engineers must identify the stakeholder needs and involve stakeholders in the definition of a concept of operations and requirements. While gathering requirements, requirements engineers must periodically ensure that operational concepts and requirements are consistent and feasible by integration. The engineers are also responsible for resolving conflicts as and when arise [4].

Stakeholders should be involved in defining the operational concepts and requirements for following reasons. First, project failure often occurs because developers are unable to acquire a detailed understanding of the user's needs, which can overcome by active participation [3, 9]. Another reason is the high level participation of customers in specifying requirements, thereby increasing the productivity more than 50% [102]. This is because the frequent communication between stakeholders and developers improves the stability of requirements [10]. In fact, the frequency of communication with the stakeholders is more important than using a requirement definition methodology, for example, performing inspections, or involving stakeholders in requirements definition teams [13]. Finally, stakeholder's participation reduces rework, avoids the introduction of unnecessary features, and better satisfies the needs of the customers [4]. Without participation of stakeholders, important needs may be ignored, and stated requirements may be incorrect, inconsistent, or ambiguous.

**Identifying the reason for developing a system**

The identification of purpose for creating a new system is one of the prime goals of requirement elicitation [7]. The product purpose is the highest-level customer requirement that identifies one or more business needs [30]. All other customer requirements must support these product perspectives. The purpose of a product enables to arise new business opportunity that necessitates a change to improve the current operation of new system, and to implement the new functionality into the system. Also, it is helpful to change user's needs, mission, objectives, environments, interfaces, personnel, or something else changed. If no such system exists then it is required to justify the development of a new system. Ultimately, systems should be able to provide a business advantage [10].

**Defining a clear project vision and glossary of requirements**

A vision statement should explain what a product will and will not do, and describe the benefits, goals, and objectives that the product will satisfy [6, 11]. Such a vision can help a team to focus on creating an outstanding product with clear benefits. The individual may be consulted from a variety of areas on a project to outline the project vision. If the individuals are unable to identify immediately the key goals and customer requirements in a just few sentence, then the project may be in trouble. This may occur because the vision is not well communicated among the team members, or the team does not agree with or believe in the vision.

Whatever is the cause, the lack of a shared vision is a fundamental flaw because its personnel lack, the overall guidance to assess the merit of features and prioritize the correction of defects. Thus, a project vision helps to resolve issues before requirements are written and shortens the requirement review process. A glossary uniquely defines the meaning of key words and phrases, which helps to avoid the misinterpretation of requirement statements. It also permits requirements to be more concisely stated.

**Identifying user roles and characteristics**

The general characteristics of the users must be accurately identified along with the process of interaction with a system [11]. General characteristics include responsibilities, education, background, skill level, activities, and modes of operation of each user role. Formal and informal interactions among the various user roles should also be described, if these are relevant to the operation of a system. Especially, it is important to establish the interaction among user groups, operators, and maintainers. Normally, users fulfil several roles, each requiring a common set of features and performing similar types of operations.

**Describing systems similar to the proposed system**

The proposed system can be described in terms of organization wide developed systems or an existing system, which is being replaced by new one. Regardless, each description should be written using terminology understandable by a typical user. More specifically, it should be free of computer jargons. Graphical representations of any kind can be used as long as they concisely describe the behavior of a system and distinguish between automated and manual processes. Each description should include the following attributes or characteristics [6, 90]:

- The provided capabilities, functions, and features.
- The adopted strategies, tactics, methods, and techniques.
- The implemented operational modes, especially degraded and emergency modes.
- Existing operating environment characteristics and interfaces to external hardware and software systems.
- All system components and their interconnections.
- All known current operational risk factors.
- Actual performance characteristics, if known. Such characteristics should consider peak and sustainable speed, throughput, and volume requirements

**Identifying all external interfaces and enabling systems**

An enabling system is anything that a system needs to perform its mission but is external to it. For example, an enabling system for JPL project is the Deep Space Network (DSN). Typical external interfaces include other database supported software and hardware such as, input and output devices [39]. Each interface and enabling system is described by its purpose, source, format, structure, content, and method of support [90,]. Context diagrams can be used to identify the external interfaces and enabling systems, with arcs that indicate events, not data flows [90, 12].

Defining external interfaces and enabling systems help to expose potential problems by revealing system boundaries, which are typically a major source of defects. When identifying external interfaces and enabling systems, a requirements engineer should determine how they can adversely affect a system across the interface as well as how they can change. For every change, the risk associated with each change should be managed.

**Emphasizing the definition of vital non-functional requirements**

Requirement engineers should pay particular attention to operational, performance, user interface, and site adaptation requirements while defining requirements. Since, it is extremely vital to the successful operation of a system, but these are often overlooked [44].

When operational requirements are defined for a product, an organization spend less time to train its users whereby users usually spend less time to perform the allotted tasks. Similarly, when requirement engineers identify specific performance requirements, project personnel can select appropriate hardware, technologies, and algorithms and validate system's performance. The important performance requirements include the speed, availability, response time, and recovery time of various software functions [45].

Requirements engineers also identify screen formats, page layouts, the content of reports and menus along with availability of programmable function keys [18]. A study reported that the prototyping of user interfaces is an important practice that can be performed during the requirements definition phase because it accepts the number of omitted requirements before product development [88]. Finally, requirement engineers should define the requirements for any data or initialization sequences specific to the provided site, mission, or operational mode and specify those features that should be modified to adapt software for a particular installation [81].

**Including specific quality and reliability targets in the requirements**

An organization must define the minimum level of quality and reliability, which might be acceptable [44, 47]. If not, it runs the risk of producing an inferior product that does not meet the needs of its customers. Similarly, organizations should define quality at least in terms of incoming defects after deployment, mean time between failures, and defect removal efficiency.

### 1.4.2. Analysis Practices

Requirement analysis is the process of identifying appropriateness, completeness, quality, and value of a set of requirements. There are following important practices for analyzing requirements such as, development of conceptual model, allocating the requirement in top-down manner, and capturing requirement rationale etc., which are discussed below.

**Develop conceptual models**

A conceptual model is an abstraction used by a software engineer to understand a system before its construction [88]. Abstraction involves the selective examination of certain aspects of the real world and desired system. Of course, what is required at any time is dependent on the needs of the system users. Abstractions may be partially incomplete and inaccurate. Hence, a good model of a system represents the aspects of a problem critical to its solution. The correspondence modeling is a latest modeling concept, which involves building models so that there could be a one-to-one correspondence between artifacts of the real world and existing models. Also, the field of artificial intelligence calls correspondence modeling based reasoning, whereas it is referred to as object-oriented analysis and design in object-oriented methodology.

There are several approaches to describe models. One of the most popular approaches is the Unified Modeling Language (UML) [90]. The UML modeling process involves several important activities such as, identification of real world concepts by examining the scenarios, using external interfaces, and enabling the systems to execute the operations. UML can also be used to specify, visualize, construct, and documents the requirements. Generally, The UML modeling process is useful to identify the relationships among the various real world entities. Also, it is useful in identifying the conception and behavior of elements, which are closely coupled with each other and grouped into single units, thereby system performance, can be visualized. Hence, UML can be described as a general purpose visual modeling language to visualize, specify, construct and document software system. Therefore, UML can also be used to model software requirements, which can help analyst to describe user requirements in more effective manner.

There are certain benefits associated with conceptual model, i.e., software engineering personnel can use a model to check the specifications and requirements of a new system. Second, software organizations can use a model to educate people and provide them with a general understanding of the structure and operation of the modeled problem domain. Third, programmers can derive working systems directly from a model. The modeling makes it easier to inject faults into software simulations, which ease debugging and testing activities. Also, it can help to identify development risks. Finally, conceptual models tend to be stable over time and can form a basis for software reuse.

**Allocate requirements in a top-down manner**

Requirements can be allocated in system components and development cycles [84]. Allocating requirements to system components is the first step in planning the development of a system. Thereafter, requirements are allocated for development cycles after requirements have been prioritized.

**Capture requirement rationale**

The rationale for each requirement explicitly states needs of stakeholders. The identification of rationale is a real statement of a desired functional requirement whereas the original statement is simply one realization that satisfies it [74]. Hence, identifying rationales is one way to find the true functional requirements. In addition, rationalization allows other people to annotate a requirement with supportive or contradictory information that can identify unrecognized issues and offer alternatives. Thus, the benefit of documenting rationales of requirements generally improves the quality of defined requirements, shortens the review of requirements, improves impact analysis, and captures corporate knowledge [64].

### 1.4.3. Risk Analysis

The common requirement risks include unknown or changed regulations and interfaces, missing requirements, technical feasibility, cost overruns, and schedule uncertainty. Consequently, when identifying requirements, engineers can identify requirements that do not have these risks as well as identifying requirements that could have significant impact in software development [58]. Once risk has been identified, project personnel are required to perform feasibility studies and risk assessments.

### 1.4.4. Specification Practices

Requirement specification establishes an understanding between customers and suppliers about what a product is supposed to do. It provides a basis for estimating costs and schedules, and provides a baseline for validation and verification [25]. The specifications are most often written in natural language [33]. The use of natural language unfortunately does not offer enough structure to produce good requirements. Hence, practitioners should adopt some practices to improve the specification of requirements. The development of good requirements requires a lot of analytic thought.

### 1.4.5. Validation Practices

Requirements validation attempts to demonstrate artifacts that satisfy established criteria and standards. For requirement engineering, validation attempts to show that requirement statements adhere to the specification practices identified earlier. System analyst should review software requirements using a defined procedure to validate the requirements accurately that reflect the needs of the stakeholders [52, 26, 27]. Although review process is unable to catch all defects, developers usually have the knowledge to interpret most requirements correctly [88, 89].

### 1.4.6. Requirement Management Practices

There are certain important practices that managers perform for planning, monitoring interactions among people, and tracking development progress. The status and change activities of each requirement must be monitored carefully in a regular interval. Further, summary data should be collected as change metrics for the total number of changes that other requirement engineers have proposed, approved, and added to the software requirements. These metrics help to identify the quality of requirements engineering activity so that the organization can improve it.

It is reported from project experiences that the changes in defined requirements relatively causes changes in project schedule [77]. Several studies also have shown that volatility in requirements accelerates inefficient production of low-quality software [68]. Consequently, requirements should be managed using a defined configuration management process, i.e., Change Control Board (CCB) and automated change control tools that manage each requirement as a separate configuration item [82, 87].

The configuration management tool permits personnel to identify, which requirements have been added, removed, or changed since the last baseline. Here, it is important to identify who has made these changes, when they were made, and the reason for preparing configuration items by managing changes in requirements through configuration management tool, so that these changes can be traced in a systematic manner.

### 1.5.RE ISSUES

Requirements engineering process starts with requirements elicitation, which is also referred to as requirement gathering. The way of gathering requirements is an important issue of requirement engineering. It is observed that requirement gathering is not performed in a well manner, failures arose considerable problems due to requirement gathering for practitioners.

Researcher observed that accurately capturing system requirements is the major factor in the failure of 90% of large software projects. Also, poor requirements management such as, bad technology, missed deadlines etc. can be attributed to 71 percent of software projects failures. The cost of such failure may be enormous. Another study found that failed or abandoned systems cost Rs.100 Billion in the software projects [23].

The fixing of mistakes at requirements gathering stage accounts for 75 percent of all error removal costs [24]. There are certain problems in requirement gathering, which are generally faced by practitioners and it is listed in Table 1.1.

The requirement gathering problems occur because communication between stakeholders is considerably challenging issue. These problems may arise because the need of organization changes with time and scope.

Table 1.1: Problem with Requirements Gathering

| | |
|---|---|
| Incomplete user requirements | Fluctuating requirements |
| Incomplete domain knowledge | Poor users' collaboration |
| Incorrect requirements | Ambiguous requirements |

| Unnecessary design considerations | Different views of different users |
|---|---|
| Unfixed requirements | Unorganized bulky information sources |
| Over-commitment by sales staff | Too many requesters |
| Misunderstanding of system purpose | Continuous acceptance of additional requirements |

### 1.5.1. Requirements Gathering Techniques

There are various techniques suggested for requirements gathering and analysis, and these are interview, survey, questionnaires, brainstorming, prototyping, observation etc., which are shown in Table 1.2. The selection of appropriate requirement gathering techniques is important task, which should be carried out according to the type and complexity of the project. Here, different techniques for requirement gathering are provided with their pros and cons.

Table 1.2: Requirement Gathering Techniques

| Interview | Survey |
|---|---|
| Questionnaire | Brainstorming |
| Group work | Joint Application Development (JAD) |
| Prototyping | Requirement workshop |
| Observation | Protocol analysis |

**Interview**

An interview is an effective requirements gathering technique in which the requirements are elicited through face-to-face conversion with the customer. Interview is verbal exchange of information between two or more people for the principle purpose of gathering information from the stakeholders. There are various categories for interviews in different ways. Generally, interviews are often categorized in relation to their structure such as, structured, semi-structured and unstructured [57].

**Surveys**

The survey is used to conduct requirement gathering over a large population of interest. This technique covers the whole geographical region to collect the large set of requirements, which is mostly appropriate for general purpose software development. The response rates can vary from 1% (charity survey) to 95% (census survey) [87, 90]. It is used to collect information from a large number of users simultaneously and if it is designed correctly, it can be quick and easy to analyze the data. However, it has some disadvantages, i.e., rich data collection is not possible, and it does not provide the holistic view of a system.

**Questionnaires**

Questionnaires are used as a simple tool, which may consist of open and/or closed questions [87]. The questionnaires must be clear, defined and concise with respect to the domain of the system to be developed, so that the right result and response can be observed. Questions must focus on the problem. The redundancies in the questions must be avoided. Questionnaires provide an efficient way to collect information from multiple stakeholders quickly. Generally, questionnaires are considered more useful as informal checklists to ensure fundamental elements are addressed early on, and to establish the foundation for subsequent elicitation activities. In addition, it has some deficiencies, i.e., questionnaires lack the opportunity to investigate further on a topic or expand new ideas. Also, it is unable to provide mechanism for the participants to request clarification or correct misunderstandings.

**Group Work**

In the group work, different stakeholders are invited to conduct group meeting in collaboration to elicit requirements of the system to be developed [15]. It is a mostly used technique but it needs a lot of exercise to conduct. This technique is very much effective to resolve the conflicts among customers in order to bring them at one table. Each and every aspect of requirements is discussed and proper suggestions are provided using group work. In group work, the stakeholders provide the direct remarks about the software requirements. In continuation, it has some disadvantage such as, lot of effort is required as compared to other requirements engineering techniques. Sometimes all the stakeholders can join at the same time as it may be possible that members may be busy in other tasks. Group work is less effective in the highly political tense situation.

**Brainstorming**

Brainstorming is a process, where participants from different groups of stakeholders engaged in an informal discussion to rapidly generate as many ideas as possible without focusing on any one in particular [51]. So much severe criticism is not allowed in brainstorming because the biasness can be generated. The ideas are freely explained and everyone has to interpret it in a very pleasant environment with some informal discussion. Brainstorming is seriously affected by requirements specification process. But brainstorming is mostly used for the innovative sort of projects, where each participant provides his or her own ideas after their personal research about the project to be started. Brainstorming is often used in decisions making about the requirements of the project. It promotes free thinking and expression of ideas.

**Joint Application Development (JAD)**

Joint Application Development (JAD) is a combined business analysis approach that solves a problem in which large numbers of stakeholders are interested [52]. This approach is mostly used for agile software development in which the quick amounts of requirements are elicited [20]. JAD provides the rapid decision making about the problem and its solution. It handles the rapid changeability in requirements. Also, it provides well formatted structured approach for requirement gathering. Further, it provides the direct communication between all stakeholders of the project. As JAD provides rapid solution, sometimes it is unable to provide the exhaustive validation in least amount of time. JAD team does not have huge experience and expertise in the problem domain.

**Requirement Workshops**

Requirement workshop is a collection of different types of meeting conducted by the stakeholder to elicit the requirements of the project [53]. This technique provides a complete set of requirements as compared to brainstorming and group meetings. Requirements are mostly unchanged, whenever elicited with this type of method. Therefore, requirement workshop is feasible for the large and complex solutions.

**Observation**

It is one of the ethnographic technique in which the requirement engineer visits and observes the environment of the customer at client site. This technique is often used in conjunction with interview and task analysis. Observations are highly authentic requirements engineering tool because the requirement engineer by himself observes the whole environment of the customer. It is mostly used in order to validate and verify the requirements. In addition, observations are very much expensive to be performed because of the travelling costs. Also, results of observations are wrong as the customer problems are difficult to understand as these are being watched during observations and adjust themselves.

**Protocol Analysis**

Protocol analysis is a type of meeting, where participants discuss the requirements of the customer noisily. Protocol Analysis also provides the required actions to be taken for fulfilling users' requirements using Rationale Rose [14, 18, 21]. It can provide specific information and rationale to analyst for the processes that is supported by target system. Protocol analysis enables all the stakeholders to provide active participation. Sometimes, it does not provide the true picture of the requirements as discussion through operations.

**Prototyping**

Prototype is a model of a final product introduced into market to provide services to the customers. Through prototyping, the customer can gain the experience and also may be able to provide other requirements that need to be implemented in the next prototype. The feedback from the users is recorded in the form of system requirements [56, 71]. The prototyping provides the detailed information by examining each prototype by the customer. It is mostly used in conjunction with other elicitation techniques such as, interviews and JAD. Prototyping is useful while developing human computer GUI interfaces. Also, prototypes provide a good chance to the stakeholders to express their needs to the stakeholders. Despite of these advantages, prototypes are expensive in terms of time and cost. Another problem in prototyping is that the user often resists making changes if once they became experienced. Among all above requirement gathering techniques, the selection of an appropriate technique depends upon the type and complexity of the project to be developed. If the project is related to the market survey, it can be the best technique. The interview is the most suitable techniques for the projects specific to the particular organization. However, the selection of technique is decided by the analyst based upon project nature. The research emphasized mostly on interview techniques, which is discussed in the subsequent sub-sections.

### 1.5.2. Conducting Interviews

The various important research works have been carried out in conducting interviews [47]. There are three main types of interviews, namely; structured, semi-structured and unstructured. In structured interview, all the questions are closed ended and the respondent is not allowed to speak beyond the context and scope of the project. The responses are predefined here. This type of interview is preferred for the collection of quantitative data. The structured interviews allows for interview with multiple interviewees, the data collected is more closed to the population oriented and is easier to analyze. The interviewer has more control over interview by asking the questions in a specific order. In a semi-structured interview, the interviewer usually asks some predefined questions and also other spontaneous questions to find out the interests of the respondent. The questions prepared in advance set the guidelines for an interview. Also, quantitative data can still be collected using pre-defined questions.

Unstructured interviews are informal interview without restriction about the scope and context of the topics called. There are no predefined questions prior to interview. The unstructured interview is conducted in a more conversational manner. There is a limited control over such kind of interview and the data collected is totally qualitative and is difficult to replicate. Unstructured interviewing can be a time consuming way to generate data and there is greater potential for interviewer bias. It is observed that structured interviews gather more information as compared to unstructured interviews. Unstructured interviews collect more information than sorting and ranking techniques.

A research work on requirement gathering found that the interviews can be the most effective way to obtain requirements. For that, around 32 online databases is explored including ABI/Inform Global (ProQuest), Academic Research Library (ProQuest), Australian Public Affairs (APAFT), Full Text (Informit), Business Source Premier (EBSCO), Communication and Mass Media Complete (EBSCO), Emerald Management Xtra (Emerald), Expanded Academic ASAP (Gale), Factiva, ACM library and the IEEE Library. In addition, some thesis materials were also retrieved from Google scholar, which were not available in the databases. A search was made for refereed articles using the keywords requirements, information system requirements, requirements analysis, information systems with dialogue and interview. This has returned around 33 references. Around 18 research papers were extracted to determine, which references were concerned with original research into requirements gathering through interview. Each paper was then checked to verify references that had not already included in the list of research. The research reported was intended to be collated using the same method. It was found that there were no research outputs that had been replicated by independent teams. Many authors purport to be talking about requirements gathering, but quickly gloss over the issues and then perform research on one of the requirements analysis techniques. Therefore, more emphasis must be given on interview technique, which is most applicable in requirement engineering practices.

Here, a four segment interview model is presented to illustrate effective requirement gathering process as shown in Figure 1.1. The interview model can be useful for conduction of effective face-to-face interaction between analyst and user in order to elicit requirements. The model has four segments, i.e., conspicuous requirements, user knowledge, analyst knowledge and mutual understanding between user and system analysts.

The conspicuous requirements can be shared by user and analysts, whereas the user knowledge and analyst knowledge are required to exchange between these stakeholders for imperative requirement gathering. Also, the mutual understanding between stakeholders can overcome the conflicts that arise in interview process. The segments of the models are described in the subsequent paragraphs.

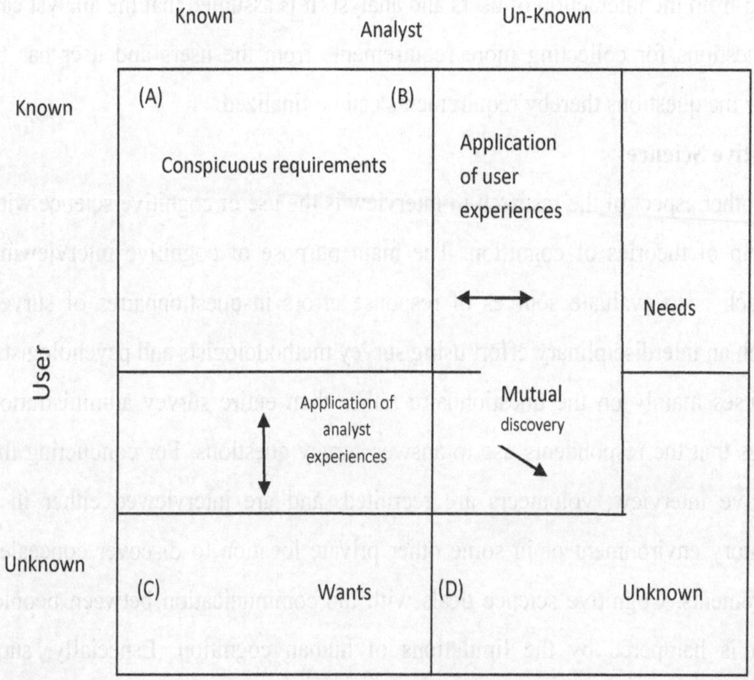


Figure 1.1: Interview Model

Segment A represents the knowledge, which is common to both analyst and users. Repeated interviews would hope to increase the size of this quadrant. The Segment C represents the knowledge that the analyst has but users do not have. It includes knowledge of the analyst skills as well as the knowledge gained from education and training. By making use of this knowledge, analyst will be able to provide the product knowledge. The knowledge that the user has but the analyst does not have, is represented in Segment B. It includes understanding of the unique business models of the users business. The analysts try to learn such knowledge from users. The Segment D represents new knowledge that will be created from the interaction of users and analyst. It is assumed that the analyst can ask questions for collecting more requirements from the users and user has to answer the questions thereby requirements can be finalized.

**Cognitive Science**

Another aspect of the research in interview is the use of cognitive science with the help of theories of cognition. The main purpose of cognitive interviewing approach is to evaluate sources of response errors in questionnaires of survey through an interdisciplinary effort using survey methodologists and psychologists. It focuses mainly on the questionnaire rather than entire survey administration process that the respondents use to answer survey questions. For conducting the cognitive interview, volunteers are recruited, and are interviewed either in a laboratory environment or in some other private location to discover concealed requirements. Cognitive science deals with the communication between people, which is hampered by the limitations of human cognition. Especially, such communication problems arise when it needs to be conducted by language. The communication problems can be classified as the limitations of humans' cognition as information processors, the complex nature of requirements, and the obstacles encountered in user and analyst interaction [45].

The research reported that interaction obstacles in cognitive interview can also be characterized by internal company policies and by external customer characteristics. There is also some research work carried out on language difficulties, which is arising because of varying software development terminology [75]. The most fruitful outcome can arise by applying theory of individual cognition to improve conversational performance and increase the ability to requirement gathering. An important issue of requirement gathering is the lost relationship between customer and developers. It results poor requirement gathering process that causes the software project failures [85].

Some researchers have found that there is absolutely lack of attention among experts about the way they elicit the information or knowledge [88]. An effective relationship was discovered between behaviors of the stakeholders and high quantity learning outcomes [87, 88]. Teaching approaches were designed to encourage successful learning behaviors. A strong relationship was found from stakeholder's experiences, the nature of learning, and the value of learning outcomes. Based on the findings of this research, it is found that the improved understanding of requirements gathering conversations can be obtained by cognitive interview approach.

### 1.5.3. Participation Difficulties

Requirement specification is an important dimension of requirement engineering process, which is based on domain understanding, i.e., organizational, technical, functional, and social domain. Ideally, the requirements engineers are selectively engaged in distribution of knowledge within the team, which cover all aspects of the corresponding domain [82]. However, this happens rarely because of knowledge deficits in most organizations due to lack of communication between stakeholders [10]. In general, individual members do not have all the knowledge required for the project and they must acquire additional information before accomplishing productive work [79]. Knowledge acquisition and sharing can only be achieved through effective participation between the various stakeholders. It is widely recognized that participation problems are a major factor in the delay and failure of software projects. Especially, it is true for socio-technical software systems, which must exist in a complex organizational setting. The organizational domains, where such software is introduced are often too intricate and fluid to be fully understood. In this situation, misunderstandings and conflicting views are common. There have been a number of field studies on requirement engineering related to the social-technical communication problem in software development process [20].

The presented research work focuses on the participation characteristics of the requirements engineering process. Moreover, the investigation performed not only utilized the experience of software engineering practitioners but it also reflects the views and experiences of end-users based on their recent software procurement projects. The research domain of the study was the requirements engineering phase of fully customized software development projects. The field study was conducted in two stages with the help of interviews and questionnaires.

The combinations of learning, data gathering and analysis techniques have been applied to investigate participation problems, their causes and consequences. The information was collected through literatures and empirical studies. The literatures were surveyed to find out the research problems in requirement gathering. A cross section of social science and Computer Supported Co-Operative Work (CSCW) literature was also surveyed to find the empirical results and reasoning about the possible causes and consequences of participation difficulties. There are inherent complexities in combining qualitative and quantitative methods. Therefore, empirical study was essential to avoid an unsupported assertion, which is carried out in two stages. The first consisted of informal interviews and observations to establish some knowledge about software development practices and methodologies of both developers and customers and another stage was evaluation of questionnaires' responses, which are shown in Table 1.3. In this study, 5 interview samples from software developers and user have been collected. Also, 42 questionnaires' responses from practitioners and 37 responses from users were collected.

Table 1.3: Stakeholders' Participation

| **Types of study** | **Software practitioners** | **Customers/ End-users** |
|---|---|---|
| Interview sample size | 5 | 5 |
| Questionnaires responses | 42 | 37<br>(21 participating and 16 non-participating) |

The interviews concentrated mainly on the participation channels between agents participating in any software development project as well as the problems that can be attributed to the ineffectiveness of those participation channels. Other management and technical issues such as, schedule and place of interview were also discussed. From interviews, it is found that the practitioners irrespective of their experiences, precise about facts and procedures rather than their opinions and judgments. Therefore, interviewer is unable to ask for direct judgments on hypothesis. Instead of this, each hypothesis was tested in terms of its external effects and indicators. Most of these hypotheses were turned out into the multi-dimensional solutions and thus it can be measured through various indicators.

For example, the effect of organizational power was multi-dimensional, which govern the choice participants and their working procedures. It has been tested in two separate questions, each of which had a number of variable answers. In order to get a value for the strength of feeling for each indicator, the Likert Scale method was employed [4]. Each variable was rated in five scales in relation to the other variables within the same question.

The second stage of study was based on two questionnaires; one for customer and another for the software developers. Questionnaires were collected from software industries and their responses represent a procedure of software development and interaction between stakeholders of the companies that were targeted. The questionnaires were designed to get a quantitative evaluation for various aspects of the participation activities during requirement engineering. The developers were involved in either developing a new software system or maintaining an existing one. Some of them were also involved in the provision of hardware systems.

#### 1.5.3.1. Types of participation difficulties

Large software projects suffer serious breakdown problems due to improper co-ordination and participation between stakeholders throughout their development life cycle. In this section, breakdown causes of participation during requirements engineering phase is discussed and these are one way participation channel, familiar participation, and the lost link and conflict notation.

**One Way Participation Channel**

Generally, software engineering practices use participation methodologies, which are used to convey information within the development team and with the various stakeholders. Ideally, participation channels between various communities should be perfect thereby knowledge can be shared among the stakeholders. In practice, it is expensive and time-consuming to support extensive participation between the communities, and the channels are restricted to one way participation in the form of specification documents. Some researchers have observed that the documentation has no effect for participation, as it is unable to resolve misunderstandings.

Nevertheless, an implicit over-the-wall model exists in most software development projects in which every stage provide requirement specification to the next stage to proceed for further stages [22]. The metaphorical wall is often encouraged by management among the stakeholders in large software projects for stakeholders' participation but more often it is merely a result of constraints on coordinating a large team. Thus, The SRS is the most common document in which analysts communicate requirements back to their clients for validation. The way to communicate the requirements is based on formal specification document, informal combination of documents, informal specification documents and natural language discussion, which is shown in Table 1.4. The survey results that the most convenient way for communicating requirements is formal specification documents. The 40% of users adopt this format while communicating the requirements [23]. In addition, informal specification and natural discussion such as, direct communication or face-to-face communication is less applicable. Whereas, it is important way to collect the actual requirements of users in their own assumption, is generally neglected.

It is observed that there are two standard approaches for one way communication problem. The first emphasizes on development of better notations and effective use of electronic repositories. The second concentrates on the importance of contact between development team and other stakeholders, which rise to practices such as, end-user participation and ethnographic techniques.

Table 1.4: Communication of Requirements

| Format | Using by stakeholders (in %) |
|---|---|
| Formal specification documents | 40 |
| Informal combination of documents and discussion | 30 |
| Informal specification documents | 11 |
| Natural language discussion | 19 |

Each of these approaches has its own set of problems, which directly unable to address the question of facilitating appropriate and effective participation over restricted channels.

Finally, it is found that the compromised form of enriching notations with natural language descriptions and utilizing the personal contact of face-to-face discussions is an easy way to communicate the requirements with the customers. Generally, the users are not very much aware about the product specification, for this reason the aforesaid solution can be helpful for end-users.

**Familiar Participation**

Organizational processes are generally described in terms of an organizational chart. However, the participation relationships are normally not represented in the organizational chart. Also, the organizational chart is invaluable, where it is unable to define informal relationships such as, face-to-face discussion, formal meeting etc., which is necessary exercise in every organization. The practitioners have outlined many difficulties during unexpected interactions between system elements. In spite of the time and effort spent on studying organizational structures, practitioners neglect the familiar participation among systems element. On the other hand, such informal participation channels can be destroyed by opposition and enmity, which can discourage co-operation and affect the normal flow of information. The way to exchange information between developers and end users is shown in Table 1.5. The face-to-face discussion is the most effective way to exchange user requirements whereas telephonic conversion is less usable.

Table 1.5: Information Exchange

| **Methods of Communication** | **Participation (in %)** |
|---|---|
| Face-to-face discussion | 45 |
| Formal meeting | 25 |
| Telephone conversation | 12 |
| Using documents | 18 |

**The lost link and notation conflict**

The inability to trace the sources of actual requirements and their related information is identified as requirements traceability problem [21]. Requirements traceability is vital for all phases of the software development cycle to aid reasoning about requirements and justify changes. It is observed that the traceability problem is particularly serious at the later stages of requirements engineering [20, 21]. Also, it becomes more serious when new requirements are introduced in the later stage of the project life cycle. The newly introduced requirements do not conflict with existing requirements therefore, it is necessary to re-establish participation with the human sources of existing requirements.

Generally, it is exhaustive process due to paucity of time thereby the analysts halts the communication with the end-users, which results in unexpected delay in software development. Table 1.6 presents the links that practitioners use in order to establish requirements traceability to the requirements sources. Here, it can be observed from the above results that the most analysts link the requirements to user groups and departments, which means that traceability is not directly linked. Only 15% linked the requirements to their individual sources by name, which means that those sources can be traced directly if necessary. The link to job titles might sound like a good idea, but it does not work in dynamic organizations, where people move between jobs and even move between organizations.

Table 1.6: Tracing Links for Sources of Requirements

| **Linking requirements to sources** | **Linking (in %)** |
|---|---|
| Requirements are linked to user group and departments | 65 |
| Requirements are linked to individual source by name | 15 |
| Requirements are linked to job titles of their source | 20 |

While programmers, software engineers and analysts are describing the system in terms of its procedures and data structures, end-users prefer the system in terms of its general behaviour, functionality and applications. The different communities involved in the requirement specification process prefer different types of notation, and various people may be unfamiliar with various notations. For example, a user may not be interested to understand formal specification languages, but the programmer may require these to obtain an appropriate level of detail. It is often the analyst's responsibility to choose the notations that can best describe the system for each interest group.

The chosen notations can used to explain the system differently to each group. The analyst combines the notations with explanation to make it easier to understand requirements. Typically, two types of techniques are used in such kind of notation such as, the control flow information, which might be represented by specialized notations like pseudo code and flowcharts, and another is data structure information, which might be represented using diagrams or a textual description [72]. Some software programs such as, the traditional numerical analysis systems have complex control structure with relatively simple data structures. On the other hand, traditional commercial applications have complex data structures with relatively simple control flow. In addition, natural language, program design language, flowcharts and hierarchical diagrams have been compared to define better notation regarding requirement specification. It is observed that the program design language and flowcharts are more helpful than natural language descriptions to define requirements [21, 23].

Regardless of the chosen notations, most users express their requirements in natural languages. Thereafter, analyst translates requirement statements into representational object in a domain model. Once the requirements are represented, these are presented to end-users for validation. At this stage, the analysts face another participation problem, when end-users are unfamiliar with the notation. In such case, the analyst provides user's requirements in natural languages to requirement engineer to interpret the requirement in right manner for avoiding time delay. Figure 1.2 shows the various methods for requirement representation in which time duration is described in four different time slice, i.e., always, often, seldom, and never. In addition, requirement gathering methods are denoted in terms of natural language annotation, face to face explanation, and self explanation notation.

## 1.6.IMPACT OF SECURITY REQUIREMENTS IN SRS

Many of the potential clients do not initially provide requirements to software developers with sufficient information through which they estimate reasonable cost and size of projects. SRS is a formal document, which is generally may or may not be written in computer terms. It is an effective way to elaborate user requirements in a systematic manner. Also, it is a formal document, which generally includes principle of requirements specification on which the software is to be developed.

Also, it incorporates the overall description and system features with external as well as functional and non-functional requirements. Generally, it is observed that safety and security requirements can be basic requirements to design secure software products. Further, it has been observed that these requirements are not included or partially described in SRS documents. Therefore, it is suggested that safety and security requirements can be included as requirements and it can be placed in non-functional requirement section of SRS.

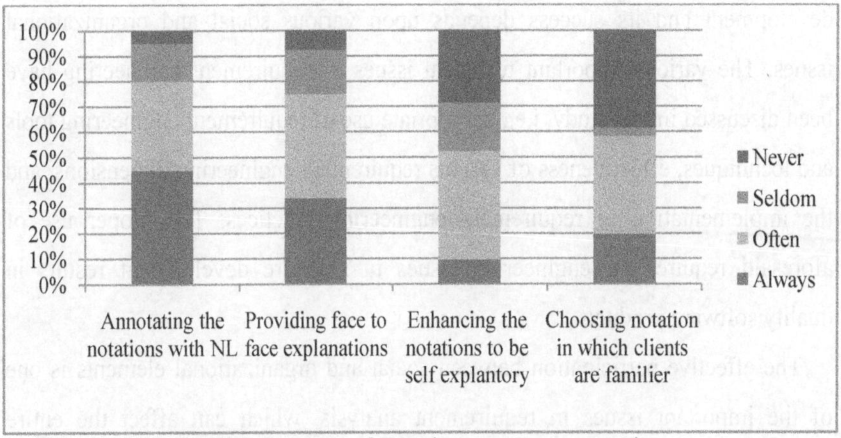


Figure 1.2: Types of Requirement Representation

The safety requirement specification is concerned with possible loss, damage, or harm. It can define any safeguards or actions that must be taken as well as actions that must be prevented. In addition, it refers some external policies or regulations that state safety issues, which can affect the product's design or use.

Security requirement specification enables to specify requirements regarding security or privacy issues surrounding the use of the product or protection of the data used or created by the product. The identity authentication of users can also be defined in security requirement specification. Also, it refers any external policies or regulations containing security issues that can protect the software products from attackers.

## 1.7.SUMMARY

There are certain serious problems associated with software development related to requirements. The research analyzes the issue and impacts of recent RE practices, which can be helpful to makes RE performance more effective. Generally, requirement engineering is an imperative stage of software development and its success depends upon various social and organizational issues. The various important technical issues of requirement engineering have been discussed in this study, i.e., appropriate use of requirement engineering tools and techniques, effectiveness of various requirement engineering dimensions, and the implementation of requirement engineering practices. The proper use of aforesaid requirement engineering issues in software development results in quality software products.

The effective participation between social and organizational elements is one of the important issues in requirement analysis, which can affect the entire software development process. One of the main reasons is that each community interprets their assumption in the light of their own words. This is especially problematic because of non-interactive participation, which can affect the effective coordination between stakeholders. Hence, it should consider as important activity, which has to be implement throughout software development process. In addition, another challenging issue in RE is to conduct interview for requirements gathering in a systematic manner to avoid software project failures. For that, we can use the personal conduct theory model and cognitive science for effective interview to collect the clear and complete requirements from various stakeholders. The impact of security requirements in SRS documents are also identified and discussed. It is observed that the security segment is normally untouched or partially included in SRS documents. Therefore, the safety and security requirements can be an important part in non-functional requirement section of SRS document, which is also discussed in the book.

Finally, some of the important issues of requirement engineering is also discussed such as, appropriate use of requirement engineering tools and techniques, role of interviews, and participation difficulties between customer and developers. The incorporation of security requirement has a great impact in SRS documents, which is also reported in the research.

# CHAPTER 2

# REQUIREMENT VALIDATION

## 2.1. INTRODUCTION

Software engineering is the application of a systematic, disciplined, quantifiable approach to the design, development, operation, and maintenance of software, and the study of these approaches; that is, the application of engineering to software. It admits the techniques and procedures, frequently determined by a software development process, with the purpose of improving reliability and maintainability of software systems. The discipline of software engineering includes knowledge, tools and methods for requirement analysis, design, construction, testing and maintenance. There are several research areas in Software Engineering such as, Requirement Engineering, Reengineering, Usability Engineering, Object Oriented Software Engineering, Client Server Software Engineering, Empirical Software Engineering, Metrics and Measurement, Usability Engineering, etc.

Requirement engineering is an important and trust research area in Software Engineering. It is the most effective phase of software development process, which involves in collecting the effective requirements from the user. The target of requirement engineering is to gather the quality requirement from the stakeholders. Also, it helps to analyze information system and planning of software systems [1, 2]. Also, it is a systematic approach through which the software engineer collects requirements from different sources and implements them into the software development processes [12]. Requirements engineering contains a set of activities for discovering, analysing, documenting, validating and maintaining a set of requirements for a system [3, 4].

Furthermore, the requirement validation is one of the research domains of requirement engineering research. It is a most important exercise to fulfil the requirement for a particular system and its main aim is to collect perfect information from the organisation/Users and then implement step by step in the correct manner. This concept implies that output of the finding is correct and it can be verified by everyone.

It is important for every organisation to develop quality software product that can satisfy user's need [13]. Checking information for its perceived correctness and completeness is a main part of the specification development process and is known as requirement validation. The successful implementation of requirement process can have a great impact on the production of quality software product.

Requirement validation examines the requirement specification to ensure that all software requirements are unambiguous, inconsistent throughout the project. It is difficult to create a reliable requirements specification because such control software tends to be highly complex. Moreover, it is well known that the majority of software errors are introduced during the requirements phase [1, 2]. To avoid problems in the latter development phases and reduce life-cycle costs, it is crucial to ensure that the specification be reliable. By reliable, we mean:

- Is the specification correct, complete, and consistent?
- Can the specification be trusted to the extent that design and implementation can commence while minimizing the risk of costly errors?

- How can we analyze the specification to prevent the propagation of errors into the downstream activities?

In this process errors have been detected and corrected; and the work products confirm to the standards established for the process, the project, and the product. The principal of requirements validation mechanism is the formal technical review. The review team that validates requirements includes software engineers, customers, users, and other stakeholders who examine the specification for errors in content or interpretation, areas where clarification may be required, missing information, inconsistencies, conflicting requirements, or unachievable requirements. System requirements specification and their validation play a key role in the development of software. It checks the correctness, completeness and feasibility criteria which will provide a great impact on the production of quality software product [14].

Requirement validation process assures that the product development team completed its task and produces a system that satisfies user needs. The software validation focuses on the method whereby the end users check the completeness and correctness of the requirements specification. User validation involves the end users of the system approving the specified system with regard to their tasks, goals and responsibilities [9, 10]. This method indicates whether the specification is complete and adequately supports the role of the users. It is important to validate with appropriate users and with an adequate range of individual reflecting the variety of roles which are to be supported by the proposed system [19]. The impact of requirement validation in software development process has very vast research scope. The validation process consists of three main steps [20]:

- The analyst chooses a set of requirements to focus the validation on particular aspect of the specification.
- The analyst defines a set of problems, each one consisting of a set of objects and a set of scenarios and problems.
- The analyst checks the defined problems and analyzes the results.

The above validation steps can be iterated arbitrarily, by correcting formalized requirement fragments and/or the corresponding categorized requirement fragments. Furthermore, if necessary, new scenarios, new properties can be created and different aspects of the requirements specification can be analyzed [18, 20]. This role of requirement validation for software development process is a very significant field of research having good amount of research work and has a great scope of software development with more reliability and satisfaction. For the successful achievement of software development process it is necessary to follow the right information, function and behaviour of the system and move forward according to fulfil the customer needs [5, 6].

From literature survey, it is found that the consistency is the main key for requirement validation in software development process [7]. At the present stage, the cost of correcting an error after delivering the system is an order of magnitude higher than the cost of correcting a similar error during the requirement analysis. So as a result it is detected that all patterns before the software development process should be properly analyze so that as a result it provide a solid foundation for software design [8].To resolve this problem, testing plays an extremely important role for requirement validation. Finding errors before they become defects will improve defect removal efficiency which reduces the amount of rework which has to be performing by software team [11]. Research indicates that the requirement validation is an important factor for software development process. Also they suggest for the basic problem occurred during software validation.

Requirement validation is the process of ensuring that the application meets functional and non-functional requirements before coding and during development. Additionally, validation is an approach, in which the analyst finds out the actual requirements before coding will start [16, 17]. Software validation takes place primarily during the system requirements analysis and design phase. There are also numerous validation techniques, including formal methods, fault injection, and dependability analysis are used and it provides security, high assurance to the required products. Requirement validation usually takes place at the end of the development cycle, and looks at the complete system as opposed to verification, which focuses on smaller sub-systems [15, 23].

Over the past 20 to 30 years, software development has evolved from small tasks involving a few people to enormously large tasks involving many people, due to this major change, requirement verification and requirement validation has similarly also undergone a change. Previously, requirement verification and requirement validation was an informal process performed by the software engineer himself. However, as the complexity of systems increased, it became obvious that continuing this type of testing would result in unreliable products. It became necessary to look at requirement verification and validation as a separate activity in the overall software development life cycle [22]. Requirement validation of today is significantly different from the past as it is practiced over the entire software life cycle. It is also highly formalized and sometimes activities are performed by organizations independent of the software developer. Hence, the requirement validation has given a substantial attention to developers and researchers for designing or planning quality software products [19, 24]. The organization of this Chapter is as follows. In section 2.2, we have discussed about the requirement validation challenges. Section 2.3 and 2.4 presents the research objective and research proposal. The line of action is defined at Section 2.5 and in section 2.6; we have studied about the background related to requirement validation. Finally, in section 2.7 we will discuss about the development of requirement validation framework (REVAF) and in Section 2.8 the outline of the Chapter is defined.

## 2.2. REQUIREMENT VALIDATION CHALLENGES

The software developer always face the problem about which requirement validation will be applied to find good and corrected requirements and what validation problems are likely to see over and over? When tackling complex validation challenges, developer will save time, money and headaches after to know the most common problems and their origin to find them. The most common requirement validation problems and challenges are:

**Missing Information**

Documents or records omitted fundamental information or content that should have been included.

**Inconsistency**

Documents contained statements inconsistent with other statements about the same topic in the same document or in the same validation package. What's more, no explanation or reason was given for the difference. We found that jargon, varying terminology, and contradictions in logic frequently caused these kinds of inconsistencies.

**Lack of Needed Detail**

This deficiency applied mostly to requirements documents. The requirements in the validation package did not adequately describe the characteristics of

- data,
- user interactions with business processes, or
- Key processes internal to the software.

**Traceability**

We found three frequent traceability problems:

- The traceability matrix did not account for a traceable specification or an observation step in a test script.
- The trace was broken. Either a requirement was barren (lacked decedents or a test) or one of the detailed requirements or test results was an orphan (lacked a parent somewhere in the requirement tree).
- The traceability matrix was incomplete. Requirement details were not explicitly numbered and traced to associated test steps. Requirements were not traced at a detailed level, so the reviewer needed to infer the detailed links between specifications and steps in a test script.

**Vague Wording**

Documents used generalities such as "in accordance to an approved procedure", or "applicable regulatory requirements", or "all associated GxP and business processes". In addition, documents used vague words such as “May”, “possibly”, “more or less”, and approximately.

**Unverifiable Test Results**

Expected results were not described sufficiently so that an independent reviewer could compare and verify actual results. The IEEE Standard for Software Test Documentation, Std. 829.1988, Clause 6.2.4 says you should, "...provide the exact value (with tolerances where appropriate) for each required output or feature". For executed scripts, actual results were not recorded or captured in a way that allowed an independent reviewer to compare them to expected results. For example, "OK" was noted in the actual-result column with no reference to a screen shot.

**GDP**

There are three frequent Good Documentation Practice problems have been found:

- Hand-recorded data and testing evidence, such as test results, were presented in a way that could cause doubts about their authenticity.
- Data that confirmed a specific requirement was hard to find in the evidence provided.
- Handwritten corrections were made that changed the sense of a requirement or an expected test result, but no discrepancy report or change request was filed. In GDP, hand corrections are allowed without additional

documentation only for obvious typographical errors, such as dropped or transposed letters.

**Incomplete Testing**

Test scripts did not fully or effectively test the associated requirement.

**Ambiguity**

Text could be interpreted more than one way, so it did not establish a single, unique requirement. The words "either" and "or" in a requirement are strong clues the text is ambiguous.

## 2.3.RESEARCH OBJECTIVES

The research objective of this research is to Design and Development of Requirement Validation Framework for Software System. Because, software systems are becoming increasingly complex and large and it is observed that there are several examples of software project failures, such as late delivery, budget overruns, and unacceptable low quality. Customers are often unhappy with the results of software products. Thus, building high quality software systems within schedule and budget is a challenge. Software development organisations are therefore recommended to improve the quality of the software development activities (software process improvement or SPI). To overcome these problems, we develop a framework for requirement validation which can fulfil the stakeholder needs and finally build a high quality software product.

## 2.4.RESEARCH PROPOSAL

The development and gathering of good requirement is the basic activity of any organization to develop quality software products. It is noticed that Requirement validation is a process that focuses on an overall objective, features, source, information, function and behaviour of the system to be built. Also, it is observed that the requirement validation is a procedure for determining stakeholder's needs during the software development process. Thus, the successful implementation of requirement process can have a good impact on the production of quality software products [21]. The analysis of requirement validation techniques helps to improve the quality of the software products as well as it satisfies the customer needs. Finally, this book will focus on following issues:

- To develop a framework for requirement validation to analyze the role of requirement validation in requirement development .It can be done by requirement analysis techniques.
- The Impact of requirement validation in software development process will define the improved the consistency and quality of the required products.
- To discover the effective techniques of requirement validation that gives a solid foundation for designing the good products for the organization/users.

## 2.5. THE LINE OF ACTION

To develop requirements validation techniques, the following requirements validation approaches will be used for effective validation of user's requirement,

- **Prototyping**: A prototype is an operational model of the application system. It helps in discussing a particular problem, clarifying a particular question, or preparing a particular decision, and thus, supplemented with written system specification.

- **Animation**: Animation of a specification is the process of providing an indication of dynamic behavior of the system by walking through a specification fragment in order to follow some scenario.
- **Reviews and Inspection**: The review process is very effective to remove unwanted and ambiguous requirements from SRS. It is a manual technique which involves multiple readers to check the omission and anomalies in the requirement document and inspection is a well-known formal evaluation process whereby a group other than authors examines the software requirements in detail in order to detect faults, infringement of development standards and other miscellaneous issues. This examination includes the detailed review of code and design as well.
- **Testing**: Testing is also a validation technique which is used to test the software requirements specification (SRS) at earlier stages before developments. In this technique, test cases are designed at the earlier stages of requirement testing to uncover the ambiguous requirements from SRS document that can be used in final requirement development.
- **Natural language paraphrasing**: Natural language paraphrasing is also a validation technique which are organized in order to tackle the problem caused by two conflicting concerns i.e. concern of the analyst to develop a formal requirements model, and the users' need to communicate their requirements in their own universal, widespread terminology.
- **Expert System Approaches**: Expert system is the method or domain knowledge of some aspects of requirements engineering process that they

represent. To assist the validation of requirements, this category of approaches includes a number of automated tools.

## 2.6. BACKGROUND STUDY

Software systems are becoming increasingly complex and large. In the software engineering literature, there are several examples of software project failures, such as late delivery, budget overruns, and unacceptable low quality [25]. Customers are often unhappy with the results of software products. Thus, building high quality software systems within schedule and budget is a challenge. Software development organisations are therefore recommended to improve the quality of the software development activities. As pointed out by Morasca [26], the phases of the software process which start early, like project management and requirements engineering, are crucial in order to construct a high quality software system.

Requirements engineering is the phase of the development process where requirements are elicited, analysed, documented, and validated [30]. Unfortunately, this field is still not mature. Many studies have shown that software projects often fail due to problems with requirements [27, 30, 28]. Frequently, analysts do not know how to write good requirements specifications. The result is incomplete, wrong, ambiguous, or badly phrased requirements. According to Boehm, "errors are most frequent during the requirements and design activities and are the more expensive the later they are removed," [29]. The high cost of errors removed in late development phases has been shown in several studies performed in the 1970s and 1980s [31]. Furthermore, requirements are prone to change and the changes can come unexpected, even during the late phases of the software development process. This may prevent projects from being successful, and meeting the customer expectations [32]. Some studies [33, 25] show that only one third of the software projects today satisfies budget constraints and is delivered on time.

Requirement validation is one of the important aspects of requirement engineering. It is concerned with checking the requirements document for consistency, completeness and accuracy. The main problem of requirements validation is that there is no existing document which can be a basis for the validation. A design or a program can be validated against the specification. However, there is no way to demonstrate that a requirements specification is correct with respect to some other system representation [1]. Therefore, requirements validation really means ensuring that the requirements specification represents a clear description of the system for design and implementation and is a final check that the requirements meet stakeholder needs. Validating such a document is the final stage of the requirements engineering.

## 2.7. Development Of The Framework

A framework for requirement validation is design, which can help the software developers to validate the actual requirements of stakeholders. In that framework, the analyst tries to understand the actual problem by collecting the actual requirement from the stakeholder. After the successful completion of elicitation process, the requirements are specified from the specific document i.e., SRS. Once the requirements are specified from the SRS document, the requirement validation process will be occurred. In the requirement validation process there are some validation approaches like prototyping, animation, inspection, review, natural language paraphrasing, expert system approaches will be executed.

## 2.8. Book Outline

The organization of chapter contains six Chapters, the Chapter 2 discuss about the review of related literature of various requirement validation techniques available in various literature. In this chapter, we will also elaborate the various validation techniques, namely, formal methods, Requirements Reviews (Inspections), Requirements Prototyping, Viewpoint-Oriented Requirements Validation, Fault Injection, and Requirements Testing. Also, the merit and demerit of each and every validation techniques is discussed. The methodology study is presented at Chapter 3.

Chapter 4 introduces the Requirement Validation Framework (REVAF); their different component along with the algorithm to design the requirement validation framework is depicted.

In chapter 5, the case study of various software development companies is presented. These companies have compared with their different validation techniques and parameter to find out the effective requirement validation techniques process, which can be used in requirement engineering process for requirement validation.

Chapter 6 finally present the concluding remarks with the contribution along with main references.

# CHAPTER 3

# RESEARCH REPORTED

## 3.1. INTRODUCTION

In software engineering, the requirements validation has very core importance. The requirements validation is very helpful to confirm that the software requirements specification (SRS) is complete and free of bugs. The requirements validation is an assurance that the software requirements document is free of unwanted requirements and completely consistent [78, 79]. In order to remove inconsistency, detect defects and make the software requirements document fully functional the requirements validation is key factor [51, 52]. All possible requirements validation techniques available in literature, i.e., requirements reviews, requirements prototyping, requirements testing and viewpoint-oriented requirements validation, which have been explained in this chapter. Also, we have described the background of requirements validation techniques and a process through which ambiguous and unwanted requirements can be removed in order to check the consistency of software requirements specification (SRS). The organisation of this chapter gives the brief introduction about requirement validation techniques and we have also discussed the general concepts about requirement validation techniques with their merits and demerits in Section 3.2 to 3.5. Finally, discussion and summary is presented in section 3.6.

## 3.2. BACKGROUND

The requirements validation techniques have an important role in software development. It is valuable factor in software development life cycle and it is very helpful to judge the proposal of system [34, 53]. The main goal of this process is to design complete correct and unambiguous software requirements specification (SRS) document so that it helps the software developer to develop a system according to needs of stakeholders.

Requirements engineering process has very important role in Requirements engineering. Requirements engineering process provide a structured set of activities through which requirements documents can be validate and maintain [35, 54, 55]. There are main five factors in Requirements engineering process such as requirements elicitation, requirements analysis, requirements specification, requirements management and requirements validation.

The requirements validation process plays an important role to identify the errors in software requirements specification (SRS) before final development of a system [35,56]. Requirements validations is final phase of requirements validation techniques and it purify the inconsistency from requirements very smoothly. It is very crucial phase which demands that software requirements specification document should be free of ambiguity, inconsistency and free of errors so that in future it provide a valuable help to developer to rectify the different problems

There are some critical reasons which force to gather efficient requirements. A study made by in 2000 by Standish group. This study showed that only in America in 2000 $192 billion was spent by software companies on those software projects that exceed their time limit and estimated budget [36]. According to Standish and different studies show there are main reasons that become more significant factors in software project failure and there are [36].

- Incompleteness in Requirements and specifications.
- Very often change in Requirements and specifications.

- User dose not participate properly in(to requirements)

To overcome different problems in requirements validation all developers must have good knowledge of requirement engineer. If they have proper background in requirement engineering then can gather proper requirements for software projects. A software engineer must have proper technical skills to deal with system and he/she should be social to interact with human stakeholders of that system [34,57,58].

The requirement validation techniques provide a very learning environment to generate and gather complete and consistent requirement to design secure and critical system [59,60,68]. In some system a minor mistake or inaccuracy cannot affordable for example if we want to develop a airline control system then there is no chance that we can take minor chance of ambiguous and incomplete requirement because there are hundreds of thousand people's life hand of this system. If we spent more time in filtration of faulty and ambiguous requirements then we can save amount of time which is hundred times less than which we spent to rectify the problem after deployment of a system [37].

Poor and bad requirements create different problems at different stages of system such as system integration, operating testing and developments. Most of time cooperation to stakeholders to validate the requirements is not favourable and this leads to bad end product. The stakeholders dyed to accept such product even that verified and tested properly by quality assure department. If problems are not addressed on initial stages then may have negative impact on schedule and cost of software projects [38, 61, 62].

The figure 3.1 shows that 56 percent bugs in a project are because of requirements validation phase. It means this phase has more importance than all other phase to find and fix errors from requirements in order to develop final product [75].

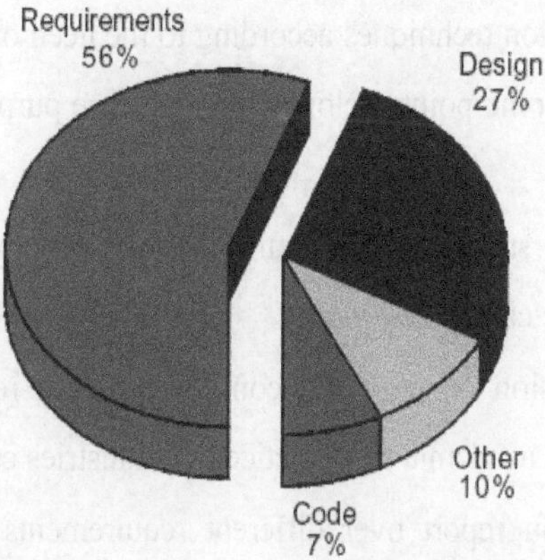


Figure 2.1: Percentage of Bugs in Software Development Cycle

## 3.3. PROBLEM DEFINITION

In today's environment mostly companies has no proper channel to validate the requirements. They are using ad-hoc based system to validate their requirements. One main reason to do so is lack of proper trained people. In these companies more focus is on testing and testing is final phase of product development. All those companies, especially small companies face lot problems in final product if there do not validation their requirements before development of projects.

The major objective of this chapter is to present a comprehensive report on requirements validation techniques used in different software organization. First we focus on all available requirements validation techniques in academia with detailed knowledge and then highlight all merits and demerits of these requirements validation techniques.

To accomplish these task different literatures such as books, articles, research papers and my personal experience of software developments have been taken. After deep study of literature, a complete and suitable method to select requirements validation techniques according to the need of a system is presented in this book. Here some points below which are core purpose to accomplish this task.

- After deep study of literature design of an informative survey questionnaire can be designed.
- Deep discussion on pros and cons of different requirements validation techniques in academia and practiced in industries can be discussed.
- A comparison report over different requirements validation techniques used in different software industries can be made.
- Suitable methods for selection of requirements validate techniques can be formulated.

### 3.4. Research Questions

- What are various requirements validation techniques proposed in literature?
- What are the merits and demerits of requirements validation techniques practiced in industries?
- What is the comparison of different requirements validation techniques practiced in industry?

The answer of aforesaid question is explained in the following sub sections.

## 3.5. REQUIREMENT VALIDATION TECHNIQUES

The requirements validation techniques provide assurance that software requirements specification is free of unwanted requirements and inconsistency. The requirements validation techniques such as, formal method, requirements reviews, requirements prototyping, requirements viewpoint-oriented, fault injection and requirement testing have been observed. The requirement validation techniques and their different aspects are discussed in following sub-sections.

### 3.5.1. Formal Methods

Formal methods are a collection of techniques rather than a single technology to apply on specifying a software system. The sole objective for using formal methods is to provide a way to eliminate inconsistency, incompleteness, and ambiguities. Because the formal methods have an underlying mathematical basis, it provides valid analysis of a system better than ad hoc reviews. There are several classes of distinguishable formal specification techniques (also called as formal methods). They are model-oriented specifications, property-oriented specifications, and operational specifications [44, 63].

In the property-oriented approaches, known as constructive techniques, one declares a name list of functions and properties. Infinite numbers of models are represented by this method because infinite numbers of functions can be provided for each of the previously declared names. Among the models, only a few of them satisfy the required properties. The software is correct with respect to a specification if it provides all the declared function names and defines a model that satisfies the specification [44]. These approaches provide notations that can depict a series of data, and use equations to describe the system behaviours rather than building a model.

These property-oriented approaches can be broken into algebraic and axiomatic specifications [45, 69]. The algebraic specification describes a system as an algebra that is consisted with a set of data and a number of functions over this set [46]. The axiomatic specification has its origin in the early work on program verification. It uses first-order predicate logic in pre- and post-conditions to specify operations [45].

In the model-oriented approach, known as declarative techniques, one builds a unique model from a choice of built-in data structures and construction primitives that the specification language offers [44]. This approach provides a direct way of describing system behaviours. The system is specified in terms of mathematical structures such as sets, sequences, tuples, and maps [45]. It defines the correctness based on the model behaviours whether it meets the specified functionality [44].

The Operational/Executable specification is another category of formal specification techniques. It provides sets of actions that describe the sequence of the system behaviour and computational formulas that describe the performance calculation.

### 3.5.2. Requirements Reviews (Inspections)

The requirements reviews is very useful and effective validation technique to find out all major defects and it was presented by Fagan in 1976 [42]. In different literature most of evidences are in favour of this requirements validation technique. According to these literatures about 60 to 90 percent defects in software requirements specification (SRS) are caught during reviews [41].

The inspection process is very effective to remove unwanted and ambiguous requirements from SRS. During this process we can detect different sort of bugs at early stage of software development that can be more expensive at later stages.[45] Mostly companies though they have limited resources are recommended to prioritize the inspection of requirements over other artefacts like for example code Inspections

**Requirements Inspection Process**

In order to complete the requirements reviews a very detail inspection process is carried out and there are different steps in this process such as planning, overview, defects detection, defects collection, defects correction. These steps are presented below in detail.

**Planning**

During the planning phase different meeting are organized and categorized the material which going to be inspect [43]. Before we present material for inspection the software requirements specifications (SRS) should be complete and free of ambiguous and unwanted requirements [43]. During planning phase different people are selected, assign them different roles and also different materials are given to them by arranging meeting schedule [43].

**Overviews**

In this phase, the writer of the software requirements specifications (SRS) presents it for other inspection team members [43]. The purpose of this phase is to presents the SRS in such way that it should be readable and understandable for other inspection team members. The writer of SRS explains it for other member in detail. This phase has some critical limitations such as it consume extra time and resources. Also this is not helpful to make consensus between inspection team members over a particular aspect of software requirements specification (SRS) [43]. These are points which justify existence of overview.

- If the inspected module is complex and difficult to understand for other team members then overview has importance.
- If inspected module is part of a complex and large system then overview phase helps to all inspector to understand the relation of this module to that system.

**Defect Detection**

In inspection process the defect detection phase has really important role [43]. In this phase all possible defects are detected from software requirements specifications. Basically there are two way to find out the defects from SRS. In first method defects are detected individually and secondly different teams are formed to inspect the requirements and highlight the possible defects. We can also eliminate the bugs by dividing this phase in to different mini phase known as Phase Inspection Method [43].

For example if we want to inspect the requirements specification of an inventory system then we will divide this phase in different inspection phase and assign two or more inspectors to each inspection phase. After a complete cycle of inspection these phase remove the bugs from requirements specifications very effectively [43, 64]. In this phase the cost of project increases at large extent.

**Defect Collection**

In this phase some points are very critical and these are listed below.

- All defects detected from requirements specifications by inspectors are collect and documented properly.
- Decision making about detected defect is it really a defect or not.
- Decision making about re-inspection of infected module

Different groups meeting are held to get the result of this phase most of meeting demanded extra time but some other meeting such as managed meeting, deposition and corresponding are held according the literature [43, 64]. Basically the three actors are involved in this meeting such as inspector, moderator and writer. Managed meetings are very formal and in depositions meetings 4 to 5 people are involved. This is not mandatory for inspector and writer to meet each other face to face they can communicate to each through email or phone in correspondence meetings [43, 64].

In this phase the capture-recapture modal used to find out the defects from requirements specification. More than one inspector can inspect the same requirements specification [48, 65]. When different inspectors inspect the same requirements specifications they have different list of bugs which detect during inspection.

**Defect Correction**

In this phase correction of defects made by writer of software requirements specifications on the base of different feedback sent by different inspection teams or inspector during inspection process. This phase make assure that all possible defects and bugs are removed from software requirements specification (SRS) properly.

**Requirements Review Reading Techniques**

Reading techniques provide very essential support to inspectors for filtration of ambiguous and doubted requirements from software requirements specifications (SRS). Inspectors use the reading techniques as a very effective strategy to simplify their workflow to purify the inconsistent requirements [43, 76]. There are many different reading techniques in literatures but practically ad-hoc reading and checklist-based are used in software industries [43, 76].

**Ad-hoc Reading Technique**

This techniques works in ad-hoc mode it mean there is no proper mechanism in this technique as its name. All members in inspection team look for unwanted requirements from requirements specification without proper direction or guidelines [43]. As such this technique is not so helpful for non experienced members. The defect correction is made on the bases of experience of inspectors [43, 76].

**Checklist Based Reading**

In this technique different questions based lists are provided to inspection team members and team members have to answer these questions which are related to consistency of requirements specifications [43]. This reading technique is very helpful for inspectors to remove loop whole requirements specification by answering different question which they forgot during inspection process [39].

**Merits & Demerits of Requirements Reviews**

The requirements review is a very effective technique to design an efficient software requirements specifications (SRS) but it only useful large scale software organization that have large number of human resources. The organizations those have large human resources they can design different team and assign them different task for inspection.

Similarly this technique is not efficient for small software organization that has short human resources. Though this techniques is most practiced techniques in software industries and recommended in literatures but still not useful for limited resources software organization [44]. In small industries this process is held by developers at some extent to validate the requirements because if they hire new team for requirements review then the cost of project increase that's why this is not in favour of small organizations [39, 67]. The following figure 3.2 shows the workflow of requirements reviews.

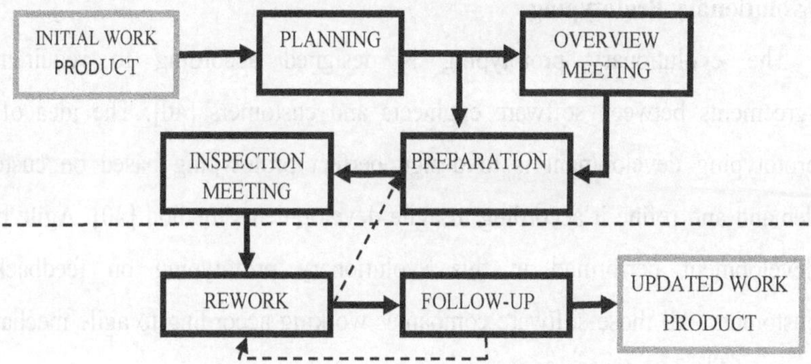


Figure 3.2: Workflow of Reviews Process

### 3.5.3. Requirements Prototyping

In requirements prototyping a software prototyping of proposed system is designed to understand the requirements according to customer needs. A well designed prototyping is helpful for software engineers to understand the behaviour of demanded software project and reduce their work by integration of the prototyping with actual system [73]. Requirements prototyping play an important role of communication agent between software developers and customers to gather appropriate requirements. When requirements from customers are gathered through requirements prototyping then its mean the customer is also part of requirements validation process [70, 71, 72]. Through working prototyping a customer can feels and see how system will behaves after developments. It is very difficult for customer to explain his all possible requirements but using prototyping it makes easy explanation for them [35, 72]. According to literature there are two types of requirements prototyping.

**Evolutionary Prototyping**

The evolutionary prototyping is designed according to requirements agreements between software engineers and customers [40]. The idea of this prototyping development is to design perfect prototyping based on customer demand and refine it according to agile developments method [40]. Agile based development performed in this evolutionary prototyping on feedback of customers. All those software companies working according to agile mechanism can use this prototyping for requirements testing.

**Throw-away Prototyping**

This prototyping is very helpful to software developer to gather consistent and smooth requirements from customers [40]. The throw-away prototyping dose not integrate to final system it is designed just to understand the customer's needs and when both software developers and customers agreed over a mutual set of requirement then discard the prototyping.

**Merits & Demerits of Requirements Prototyping**

There are some merits and demerits of requirements prototyping explained below. It is very common that to understand graphical system is easier as compare to text form. The one of the major advantage of prototyping is the customer can feels and visualize the working of their required system [39, 74]. When a software requirements document is designed by software engineers then it is difficult for customer to participate actively but they can be part of requirements gathering process through prototyping [39, 74].

It is also difficult for customer to understand the software requirements specification (SRS) of their demanded system but they can propose some new changes, correction of bugs and better user interface in requirements specification through prototyping. A proper designed prototyping can be integrated in final system to reduce work load and increase reusability. The prototyping that developed during requirements validation process can be used to validate the requirements later.

In some software industries which develop prototyping for requirements validation also used prototyping as for Alfa release when they face unexpected delay of actual system [39, 74]. When the completion of actual system finalized then this working prototyping is replaced with that system. The prototyping has some advantages but also some disadvantages as well which are explained below.

The prototyping demanded some extra resource and cost. If a company wants to design prototyping for requirements validation then they have to buy some new software and hire new people to use this prototyping. The prototyping requirements validation technique is not adoptable for small industries because it demands extra resources [39, 74].

### 3.5.4. Viewpoint-Oriented Requirements Validation

The viewpoint-oriented requirements validation technique is not so common validation techniques in literature as well in software industries. In order to understand this technique we have to go through some factors which are involved in this requirements validation technique. These factors as explained below.

**Domain of Discourse**

It deals all entities involved in software development. It define domain of information and people who are dealing with software development [47, 80].

**Actors**

All people who are participating in software development are known as actors [47]. Basically there are two types of actors who are playing their role in the development of software firstly those who are developing this system, secondly those who are using this system such as users [47].

**Viewpoint**

It means take views of all actors who are working in domain of discourse. Each and every asked for view or suggestion regarding to his area of requirements validation [47].

**Perspective**

In this factor investigate the facts by observing them into different perspective [47].

**View**

In view, different perspectives are integrated [47].

**Merits & Demerits of Viewpoint-Oriented Requirements Validation**

The viewpoint-oriented requirements validation has also some merits and demerits. This technique is very helpful to identify ambiguous and inconsistent requirements using different viewpoints. To eliminate different bugs from faulty requirements different viewpoints are incorporated. This approach to validate the requirements is not so common and almost not practiced in software industry that's way it is bit tough to highlight the core disadvantages of this validation technique.

### 3.5.5. Fault Injection

Fault injection is a technique used to observe how a software system behaves under experimentally-controlled, anomalous circumstances. Voas et al., define that system anomalies are caused by either faulty codes or corrupted inputs otherwise combinations of both. They take the approach of injecting anomalies rather than injecting faults in the software program [40, 66]. In this case study, the evaluation with abnormal inputs and outputs are covered by the test using the data item.

In this process, the system state transitions and incorrect output due to the abnormal system failures are focused to analyze. While running the simulation, either the system variables were altered or state transitions are redirected. Test cases were generated based on the functionality and significance of the failure. The fault injection is not performed to the sub module that would not cause critical system failure. In this way, the SRS is evaluated for the fault-tolerance.

At this step, simulation of the specification is used for discovering hidden faults and their location. To accomplish this, faults are injected into the model to simulate memory corruption. Four new issues arise during the fault injection process.

- Some correct inputs produced incorrect outputs;
- The State charts approach has a better chance of predicting possible faults in the system.
- During the symbolic simulation, some week points were found where faults were lurking.
- Consequently, there are many design decisions to be made in the process of developing a model (i.e., specification).

Finding the correct formulation is a process of refinement and validation, which was facilitated using this approach combined with symbolic simulation. Some requirements were found to be inconsistent / incomplete because they produced incorrect results.

### 3.5.6. Requirements Testing

A software program is tested properly using different test case before shipment to customer, but this program is tested at final stage after development. Requirements testing approach is used to test the software requirements specification (SRS) at earlier stages before developments [49]. In order to test the requirements different test cases are designed and tested. If requirement are inconsistent, ambiguous then it create problem to design test case. Most of the test cases those generated during requirement validation process are used at final testing of software. By using these test cases the work load of final quality assurance can be reduced [49].

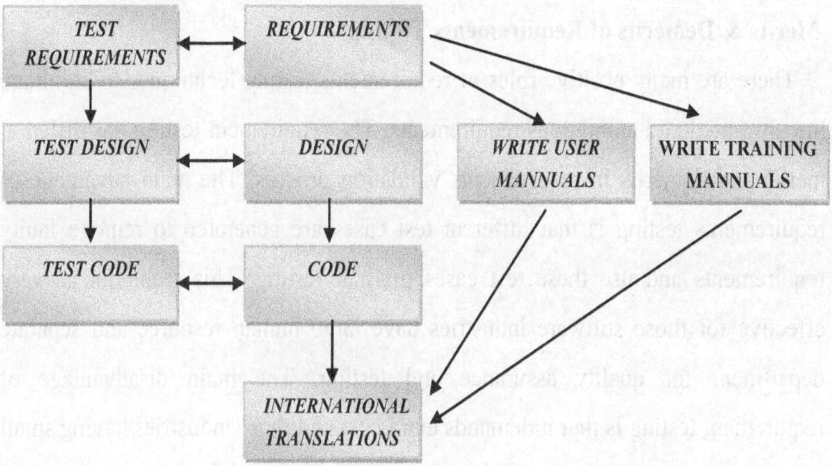


Figure 3.3: Requirements Testing

The figure 3.3 shows the requirements testing process, in which different departments are participating to design different test cases to validate requirements. The requirements testing technique demand some extra human resource such tester along with software developers. The hiring of new people in quality assurance and testing leads toward extra cost of project [77]. The inspection of inconsistent and unwanted requirements by designed different test cases known as test case driven inspection (TCD) and test case designed during

TCD inspection are reusable in different phase of software development [50]. TCD inspection has many advantages in requirements testing technique. It involves the testers in requirements validation process to reduce the work of requirements inspector [50]. Project manager can user most appropriate requirements to reduce the cost of the project Using TCD inspection.

**Merits & Demerits of Requirements Testing**

There are many positive roles of requirements testing techniques to eliminate the unwanted and ambiguous requirements. The requirement testing has different merits and demerits in requirements validation process. The main advantage of requirements testing is that different test cases are generated to remove faulty requirements and use these test cases in final testing. This technique is very effective for those software industries have large human resource and separate department for quality assurance and testing. The main disadvantage of requirement testing is that it demands extra cost and those industries having small human resource cannot get effectiveness of this technique. This technique also demands extra experienced tester and quality assurance people.

## 3.6. DISCUSSION AND SUMMARY

The requirements validation is very core and valuable area in requirements engineering. Using these requirements validation techniques the software industries can be reduce the cost of software projects and develop them according to needs of customer. These requirements validation techniques are also very helpful for software industries to remove maximum conflict at initial stage to optimize the cost and time in development of projects. It is generally accepted that, the requirement engineering is most powerful area in software engineering and requirement validation is key factor in requirement engineering. In today's life there are different requirements validation techniques practiced in software industries. Each of them has different merits and demerits of their use. Many software industries have designed proper framework architecture to use these validation techniques. Some industries are using single validation technique and some more than one. Using this framework architecture software industry can judge that they developing the system according to customer demand. The capability of requirement validation technique determine on the base defects detection at earlier stages of development but there are some other factors also important for selection suitable requirement validation techniques such as time, cost extra. Some validation techniques are very effective to find out the defects but still they are not practicable because of their other factors in many low budget software industries.

# CHAPTER 4

# REQUIREMENT VALIDATION METHODOLOGY

## 4.1. THE METHODOLOGY

To develop requirements validation techniques, various requirements approaches will be used in co-located software development. The most commonly used tools techniques are as follows, which we will use to develop the effective requirement validation framework and to identify the role and impact of requirement validation in requirement development:

- **Prototyping:** A prototype is an operational model of the application system. It helps in discussing a particular problem, clarifying a particular question, or preparing a particular decision, and thus, supplemented with written system specification.
- **Animation:** Animation of a specification is the process of providing an indication of dynamic behavior of the system by walking through a specification fragment in order to follow some scenario.
- **Review and Inspection:** it is a manual process which involves multiple readers to check the omission and anomalies in the requirement document and Inspection is a well-known formal evaluation process whereby a group other than authors examines the software requirements in detail in order to detect faults, infringement of development standards and other miscellaneous issues. This examination includes the detailed review of code and design.
- **Testing:** Testing is a requirement validation technique which is generally used in large resources company. The main aim of testing is to design test

cases at the earlier stages of requirement testing to uncover the ambiguous requirements from SRS document that can be used in final requirement development.

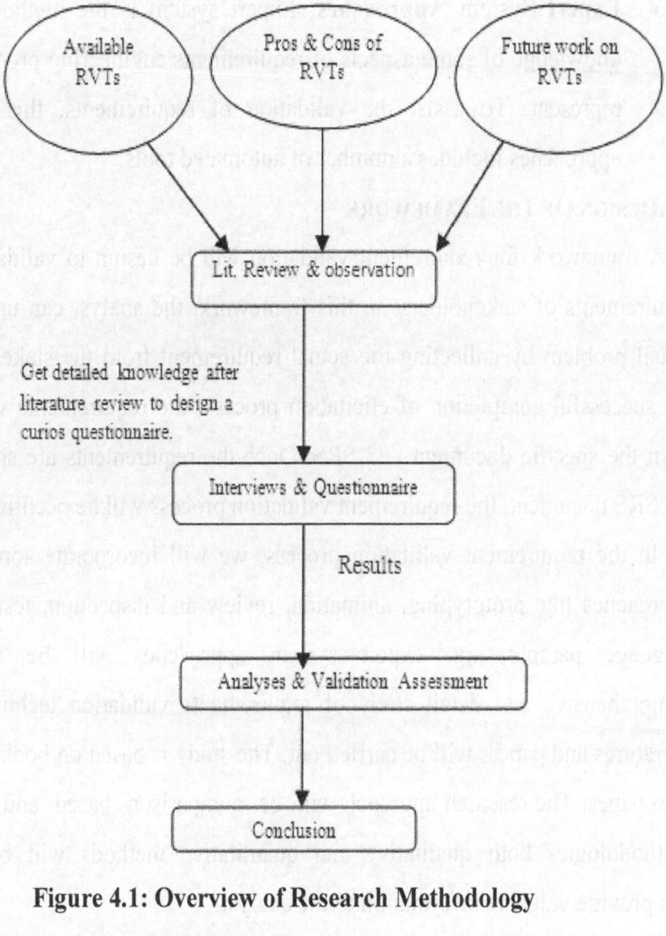


**Figure 4.1: Overview of Research Methodology**

- **Natural language paraphrasing:** Natural language paraphrasing is a validation technique which has been devised in order to tackle the problem caused by two conflicting concerns i.e. concern of the analyst to develop a formal requirements model, and the users' need to communicate their requirements in their own universal, widespread terminology.

- **Expert System Approaches**: Expert system is the method or domain knowledge of some aspects of requirements engineering process that they represent. To assist the validation of requirements, this category of approaches includes a number of automated tools.

### 4.2.DESIGN OF THE FRAMEWORK

A framework for requirement validation will be design to validate the actual requirements of stakeholders. In this framework, the analyst can understand the actual problem by collecting the actual requirement from the stakeholder. After the successful completion of elicitation process, the requirements will specified from the specific document i.e., SRS. Once the requirements are specified from the SRS document, the requirement validation process will be occurred.

In the requirement validation process, we will incorporate some validation approaches like prototyping, animation, review and inspection, testing , natural language paraphrasing, expert system approaches will be executed. A comprehensive and detail study of requirements validation techniques related literatures and papers will be carried out. The study is based on books articles and web pages. The research approach will be comparison based and in research methodologies both qualitative and quantitative methods will be used. This can provide valuable information to the analyst.

Observation of a system in real work environment is necessary for collecting valuable information about how different processes are being carried out. The analyst must observe the normal levels of supervision and control, different stages and pace of work and bottlenecks in the workflow. Although, observation is a time-consuming method, it is the best techniques to understand the system as a real world problem.

# CHAPTER 5

# REQUIREMENT VALIDATION FRAMEWORK

## 5.1.INTRODUCTION

Requirement validation is the process of conformance of stakeholder's actual requirements. There is various requirement validation techniques are available in the literature, but most of the framework do not represents the complete validation approach into the requirement engineering process. This process, verification and validation, ensures that the software conforms to its specification and that the customers ultimately receive what they ordered.

The quality of software systems depends on early activities in the software development process, of which the requirement validation is one. When requirements are not managed properly, a project can fail or become more costly than intended, and the quality of the software developed can decrease [97]. At the software development process, it is particularly important to identify all problems at the time of development phase by using techniques of requirement validation and then resolve the entire problem step by step.

For that, requirement validation techniques play a crucial role in order to construct a high quality software system. Therefore we have presented the noble approach for requirement validation process into the requirement engineering process. In this paper, we will discuss about the REVAF, their different aspects and the usefulness of the requirement validation process into the industrial setting for development of quality software products.

## 5.2. THE FRAMEWORK

In this book, REVAF is designed, which can assist the software developers to validate the actual requirements of stakeholders. In this framework, the analyst gathered and collected the requirement from the stakeholder tries to understand the actual problem. After the successful completion of elicitation process, the requirements are specified from the specific document i.e., SRS. Once the requirements are specified from the SRS document, the requirement validation process will be start. In the requirement validation process there are some validation approaches like prototyping, animation, review & inspection, natural language paraphrasing, expert system approaches will be executed. The details of the framework are elaborated in the subsequent sections.

## 5.3. STAKEHOLDERS REQUIREMENTS

Stakeholder/user requirements describe the expected services from the system, constrains on achieving them and the way the system provides the requirements. It must be written in such a way, that it must be understand by a person without technical experience and background knowledge. These requirements are generally defined using the external activities and behavior of the system and is never defined based on system design or implementation [98, 99].

## 5.4. REQUIREMENT ELICITATION

Requirement elicitation is the process of collecting the requirements. In this process the technical profession in the organization, like software developers and the system engineers, work together with the users of the system and the customers [4, 101]. This process is useful in finding the problem. Requirements elicitation phase begins with identifying stakeholders of the system and collecting raw requirements from various viewpoints.

Raw requirements are requirements that have not been analysed and have not yet been written down in a well-formed requirement notation. The elicitation phase aims to collect different viewpoints such as business requirements, customer requirements, user requirements, constraints, security requirements, information requirements, standards etc. Typically, the specification of system requirements starts with observing and interviewing people [84, 100]. So elicitation of requirement stated with the following ways: Record Inspections, Interview, and questionnaire.

### 5.4.1. Record Inspections

Organisations usually have a large volume of documents in the form organisation charts, administrative procedure manuals, standard operational procedures, policy manuals, job description documents, accounts books, sales analysis reports, etc., that can provide a valuable information to the analyst [96]. By inspecting these documents, the analyst can easily understand the working of the current system. Record inspection is the best source of quantitative information. It is carried out by the systems analyst in the following steps:

- First, the analyst visits the concerned department and meets the managers and users [96].
- He enquires various users about the documents they maintain [96].
- He identifies and prepares the complete list of documents that are relevant to the current and proposed system [96].

- He examines each and every document to understand the working of the system [96].
- In the last, the analyst collects the copies of all the relevant documents [96].

### 5.4.2. Interview

Interviews are formal meetings with current users of the existing system and potential users of the proposed system. The users may be managers or others employees of the organization, who can provide information about the working of the existing system and can explain the drawbacks of the current system.

Although, an interview is a time consuming method, it is the best technique for getting the qualitative information. Interviews must be conducted in a planned way [81]. They are carried out by the systems analysts in the following steps:

- First of all, the analyst decides the objectives and also describes the purpose of the interview.
- The analyst identifies the users to be interviewed.
- He/she establishes a mutually convenient time, duration and place for meeting with each user in advance.
- The analyst obtains the appropriate manager's consent before interviewing staff.

### 5.4.3. Questionnaire

It is a structured and formal method of collecting data. It is mainly used, when there is a scattered group of users and it is not possible to conduct interviews of all the users. It allows the analyst to obtain information from a large number of persons without conducting interviews. Questionnaire could be open-ended or closed. In open-ended questionnaire, questions are given without any choice of answer and the user has to write the answers in own words on the space given. In closed questionnaire, a choice of answers is given with each question and the user has just to mark the correct response. The data collected through questionnaire can be used to analyse the obtained results.

The main purpose of requirement elicitation is to gather the requirement before the product is developed. But it is difficult to discover the additional requirements until it comes in to usage or somebody is actually using it [82].The process of gathering the requirements from the stakeholders and the end users is limited and it is difficult to discover their expectations and the requirement on the new product without providing some model that resembles the appearance of the real product.

## 5.5. Requirement Specification

Requirements specification document is produced after the successful identification of requirements. The document describes the product to be delivered rather than the process of its development. Software requirement specification (SRS) is an effective tool for requirement specification which is a complete description of the behaviour of the system or software to be developed. It includes a set of use cases that describe all the interactions that users will have with the system/software [99, 83].

In addition to use cases, the SRS also contains non-functional requirements. Non-functional requirements are requirements which impose constraints on the design or implementation. SRS is a comprehensive description of the intended purpose and environment for software under development. The SRS fully describes what the software will do and how it will be expected to perform. An SRS minimizes the time and effort required by developers to achieve desired goals and also minimizes the development cost.

A good SRS defines how an application will interact with system hardware, other programs and users in a wide variety of real-world situations. Parameters such as operating speed, response time, availability, portability, maintainability, footprint, security and speed of recovery from adverse events are evaluated in SRS.

The Requirements specification document 'acts as a cornerstone for the entire software development process" [99]. The implications of an Inadequate Specification (in tern of errors) are now recognised and causing much concern in the software industry.

It has been claimed that "the successful design of an information system depends on the accuracy of its requirements specification" and that the poor specification of requirements is a major reason why computer system fail [73]. Checking information for its perceived Correctness and completeness is therefore an important mechanism in the construction of adequate requirements process is known as validation.

Validation ensures the accuracy of the findings of the Requirements Analysis and therefore confidence in the specification. Validation also facilitates the flow of information between the stakeholders and the system analyst. Fickas states the production of the Specification is –not so much a translation process as an interactive problem solving process". The validation procedure varies in tern of the representation format adopted to present the requirements to the users.

### 5.6. Requirement Validation And Their Techniques

Requirement validation is a most important exercise to fulfil the requirement for a particular system and its main aim is to collect perfect information from the organisation/Users and then implement step by step in the correct manner. This concept implies that output of the finding is correct and it can be verified by everyone.

Requirement validation examines the requirement specification to ensure that all software requirements are unambiguous, inconsistent throughout the project.

It is difficult to create a reliable requirements specification because such control software tends to be highly complex. Moreover, it is well known that the majority of software errors are introduced during the requirements phase [1, 2]. To avoid problems in the latter development phases and reduce life-cycle costs, it is crucial to ensure that the specification be reliable.

Requirement validation is an important activity because errors in a requirements document lead to extensive rework costs when they are ultimately discovered during development or after the system is in service. Hence, the main aim of requirement validation is not to prove the requirements correct, but instead to identify and correct all the errors. To validate requirements, various requirements techniques are available to help analyst in validation the requirements. Some of the validation techniques is as follows:

### 5.6.1. Prototyping

A prototype is an operational model of the application system [85]. It helps in discussing a particular problem, clarifying a particular question, or preparing a particular decision, and thus, supplemented with written system specification [86, 87].

It serves as the basis for discussion. In collocated context, different stakeholders communicate with each other through informal ways quickly by using prototypes that becomes more complex in global context. By using prototypes, requirements related communication can be done through normal channels to get the optimal results. But the frequency of formal interaction decreases with the increase of distance so formal communication is less significant.

Synchronous communication is a way to achieve similar level of contact as face-to-face communication consequently it seems to be most significant in Prototyping. But time zone decreases the overlapping time to bring synchronous communication effectively and commonly. As compared to this, asynchronous communication e.g. email makes it difficult to explain the requirements in order to manage the conflicts or problems.

### 5.6.2. Animation

Animation of a specification is the process of providing an indication of dynamic behavior of the system by walking through a specification fragment in order to follow some scenario i.e., its provide a powerful way of demonstrating errors, which will helps to provide a more precise characterization of each problem[86,88,89]. This technique of requirement validation can convey objectives of users to the teams that helps them to find out the locations easily where errors or misconception occurs.

In Animation, all the major aspects of requirements model is determined by giving it motivation that give a response in result. Requirement model is itself the principle media of communication. But to support the collaboration of remote stakeholders, an integration of computer technologies is used for communication which shows more significance of synchronous communication in Animation. Occurrence of formal mode of communication is, however, of least significance because it is not convenient for stakeholders, to do routine meetings as in co-located sites.

Asynchronous communication is the dominant tool in exchanging documents because it provides record and history of issues related to requirements find during validation. But its lack of interactivity lowers to handle ambiguity or other important issues relating to requirements. Hence, asynchronous communication seems to be less significant in animation.

### 5.6.3. Review and Inspection

Review is a manual process which involves multiple readers to check the omission and anomalies in the requirement document [87, 91]. The requirements review is very useful and effective validation technique to find out all major defects. In different literature most of evidences are in favour of this requirements validation technique. According to these literatures about 60 to 90 percent defects in software requirements specification (SRS) are caught during reviews [92].

In order to complete the requirements reviews a very detail inspection process is carried out and there are different steps in this process such as planning, overview, defects detection, defects collection, defects correction.

Inspection is a kind of reading/inspection technique that tries to find in the software artifacts by using formal procedures and a structured reading/inspection of the software artifacts. The terminology is not always clear when it comes to inspections. Inspection is a kind of review technique, but it is not clear how it differs from other review processes such as walkthrough or a management review. Fagan says that an inspection shall have formal procedures and produce a repeatable result [90, 91].

Inspection is a well-known formal evaluation process whereby a group other than authors examines the software requirements in detail in order to detect faults, infringement of development standards and other miscellaneous issues. The inspection process is very effective to remove unwanted and ambiguous requirements from SRS. During this process we can detect different sort of bugs at early stage of software development that can be more expensive at later stages [91].

Mostly companies though they have limited resources are recommended to prioritize the inspection of requirements over other artefacts like for example code Inspections. According to IEEE Std. 1028-1997 "An inspection is 'a visual examination of a software product to detect and identify software anomalies, including errors and deviations from standards and specifications'".

### 5.6.4. Requirements Testing

Requirement testing is one of the most important validation techniques, which are generally, practiced in large resources companies. In this technique, test cases are designed at the earlier stages of requirement testing to uncover the ambiguous requirements from SRS document that can be used in final requirement development. During this technique, developer can easily identify the conflict in SRS documents and thereafter, remove those conflicts efficiently.

### 5.6.5. Natural Language Paraphrasing

Natural language paraphrasing is a validation technique which has been devised in order to tackle the problem caused by two conflicting concerns i.e. concern of the analyst to develop a formal requirements model, and the users' need to communicate their requirements in their own universal, widespread terminology [93, 94]. It is significantly affected by control. The problem of control can arise when misunderstandings occur after the paraphrasing of model into natural language [92].

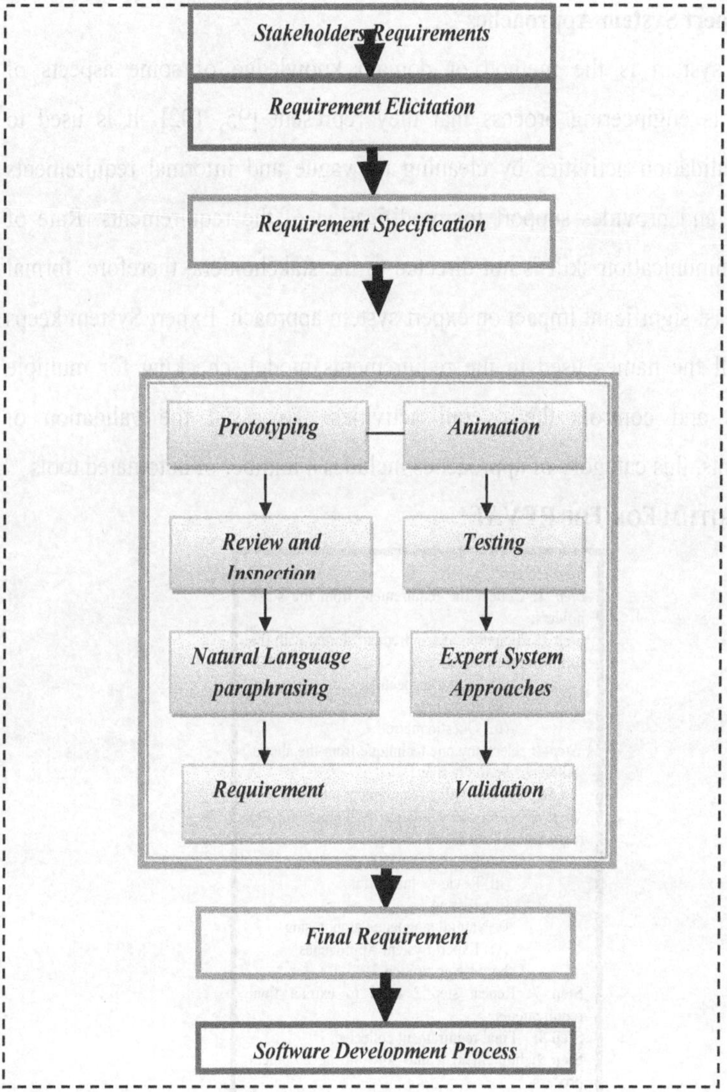


Figure 5.1: The Framework

### 5.6.6. Expert System Approaches

Expert system is the method or domain knowledge of some aspects of requirements engineering process that they represent [95, 102]. It is used to perform validation activities by cleaning up vague and informal requirements statements and provides support for modification of the requirements. Rate of formal communication skill is not directed to the stakeholders; therefore, formal way has least significant impact on expert system approach. Expert System keeps track of all the names used in the requirements model, checking for multiple definitions and controls the overall activities. To assist the validation of requirements, this category of approaches includes a number of automated tools.

## 5.7. ALGORITHM FOR THE REVAF

***Step 1*:** Start.
***Step 2*:** Collect the requirement from the stake holders.
***Step 3*:** Elicitation of requirement started with the following techniques:
(i) Record Inspection.
(ii) Interview.
(iii) Questionnaire.
***Step 4*:** select any one technique from the above, otherwise go to the step 1.
***Step 5:*** Specify the requirement into SRS.
***Step 6:*** Select the validation techniques for the requirement with the following:
(i) Prototyping, (ii) Animation,
(iii) Review / Inspection,
(iv) Testing,
(v)Natural language Paraphrasing,
(vi) Expert System Approaches.
Otherwise go to Step 5.
**Step 7:** Repeat step 2 to 6 to extract final requirements.
**Step 8:** Final requirement collected.
**Step 9:** Implement it into software development process.
**Step 10:** End.

**Figure 5.2: Algorithm for the REVAF**

The algorithm presents the process of requirement validation to validate the SRS templates. This process will start with collecting and eliciting the requirements from the stakeholders. The analyst can select the different validation techniques to extract final requirements. When the accurate requirements are gathered, analyst implements it into the software development process.

## 5.8. DISCUSSION

We have observed, that the available requirement validation models do not provide the complete features of the requirement validation techniques therefore that model will not be beneficial for the large software development process. To overcome this we have develop the aforesaid model which will provide the complete requirement validation approach into the requirement engineering process. This model can be used by those organizations that develop the large project having large amount of the data set and databases.

## 5.9. SUMMARY

The main goal of requirement validation is to meet the degree of end user's satisfaction in minimum cost and time. In this paper, the framework for this model is developed, their different component is elaborated, and the algorithm for requirement validation is also incorporated in this paper. By applying our model, software developer can develop the quality software which completely meets out with the user's requirement.

# CHAPTER 6

# CONCLUSION & RECOMMENDATIONS

The Book on "Requirement Validation: An Introduction" covers all aspects of requirement validation approach such as, the framework for requirement validation, the role and impact of requirement validation in software development process and related literature. This summary of the presented research is described in following paragraph.

- Various literatures on requirement validation have been surveyed and found there are various requirement validation approaches are available which have system analysis to maintain the SRS. Also we have explained various requirement validation practice and the methodologies related to requirement validation practice.
- The framework for requirement validation is presented, which can assist the software developer to validate the actual requirement and finally provide the quality software product as per stakeholder's need. This framework will help for those organizations which can develop large the large project.
- The effectiveness of REVAF approach with comparison to other requirement validation techniques is analyzed and found that the proper implementation of the requirement validation framework will assist the software organization to maintain and update the SRS as per software requirement.

In final conclusion, we have indentified that the requirement validation is valuable factor in software development life cycle and it is very helpful to judge the proposal of system.

The fundamental goal of requirement validation process is to design complete, correct and unambiguous software requirements specification (SRS) document so that it helps the software developer to develop a system according to needs of stakeholders.

Furthermore, the research work can be extended in the following areas:

- Automating the translation to formal model.
- Optimizing the core validation via model-checking.
- Rendering the raw output of the model-checker into a graphical, easy-to-understand format for the targeted end-user.
- Generating and executing automatically test-cases on top of the validation results obtained by the model-checker.

## BIBLIOGRAPHY


[1]. D.M. Berry, B. Lawrence, "Requirement Engineering", IEEE Software, Vol.15,No. 22, pp.26-29, 1988.

[2]. J.C. Leite, "A Survey on Requirement Analysis", Advanced Software Engineering Project Technical Report RTP-071, University Of California at Irvine, Department of Information and Computer Science,1987.

[3]. J. Siddiqi, Requirement Engineering: "The Emerging Wisdom", IEEE Software,pp.15- 19, 1996,

[4]. D. Pandey, U. Suman, A. K. Ramani, "Impact of Requirement Engineering Practices in Software Development Processes for Designing Quality Software Products", National Conference on NCAFIS, DAVV, Indore, 2008.

[5]. B. Nuseibeh and S. Easterbrook. "Requirements engineering: a roadmap". In Proc. of the IEEE Int. Conf. on Soft. Eng. ICSE, pp 35–46, 2000.

[6]. Romi Satria Wahono, "Analyzing Requirement engineering Problem", IECI Japan workshop, Japan, pages55-58, 2003.

[7]. B. Boehm, and A. Egyed, "Software Requirement Negotiation; some lessons taught", Proc. Intl. Conf. Software Engineering, ACM/IEEE, pp.503-506. 1988.

[8]. M.C. Donaldson, and M. Donaldson, "Negotiation for dummies", IDG Books Worldwide, 1996.

[9]. K. Paul, "Process Centered Requirement Engineering", England, 1996.

[10]. C. Potts, "Determining Requirement for Evolving System", Tutorials notes and slides, CAiSe'97, Barcelona, Spain, June 1997.

[11]. John, Rushby, "Formal Methods and the Certification of Critical Systems", SRI-CSL Technical Report, 1993.

[12]. D. Pandey, U. Suman, A. K. Ramani, "An Effective Requirement Engineering Process Model for Software Development and Requirements Management", International Conference on Advances in Recent Technologies in Communication and Computing, India 2010.

[13]. R. S. Pressman, "Software Engineering", A Practitioner's Approach. Sixth Edition, McGraw- Hill Inc, International Edition 2005.

[14]. D. Pandey, U. Suman, A. K. Ramani, "Design and Development of Requirements Specification Documents for Making Quality Software Products", National Conference on ICIS, D.P. Vipra College, Bilaspur, 2009.

[15]. A. Moreria. J.Araujo, and I. Brito, "Crosscutting Quality Attributes for Requirement Engineering", SEKE2002: Fourteenth International Conference on Software Engineering and Knowledge Engineering, 2002.

[16]. Ivan J. Jureta, John Mylopoulos, St´ephane Faulkner, "Analysis of Multi-Party Agreement in Requirements Validation", 2007.

[17]. Y. Yu, C.S. do, J.P. Leite, and J. Mylopoulos, "From Goals to Aspects: Discovering Aspects from Requirements Goal Models". The 12th IEEE International Requirements Engineering Conference, 2009.

[18]. M. Jackson, Software Requirements & Specifications- "A Lexicon of Practice", Principles and PreJudices. Addison-wesley, 1995.

[19]. Eushiuan Tran, "Dependable Embedded Systems", Carnegie Mellon University, 18-849b, 1999.

[20]. K. Weidenhaupt, K. Paul, M. Jarke, and P.Haumer, "Scenario Usage in System Development: A Report on Current Practice", IEEE Software, Vol. 15, no.2, pp.34-45 mar.1988.

[21]. P. Zave, "Classification of research efforts in requirements engineering". ACM Comput. Surv., 29(4):315–321,1997.

[22]. Farzana, Yousuf, Zahid Zaman, Naveed Ikram, "Requirements Validation Techniques in GSD: A Survey", 2009.

[23]. Cockburn, "Writing Effective Use Cases", Addison- Wesley, 2001.

[24]. R. Lutowski, "Software Requirements", Auerbach Publications, Boca Raton, 2005.

[25]. C.A. Dekkers, "Creating Requirements-Based Estimates before Requirements Are Complete Cross Talk", the Journal of Defense Software Engineering (Apr 2005) 13–15, 2005.

[26]. S. Morasca, 2001. "Software Measurements in Handobook of Software Engineering and Knowledge Engineering", 1, World Scientific Publishing Co. Pte. Ltd, 2001.

[27]. I. Bray, "Introduction to Requirements Engineering", Addison-Wesley, 2003.

[28]. M.A. Dennis, "The Standish Group. The CHAOS Report": The Standish Group, 1994.

[29]. B.W. Boehm, R.K. McClean, and D.B. Urfrig, "Some Experience with Automated Aids to the Design of Large-scale Reliable Software". In Proceedings of the International Conference on Reliable Software (Los

Angeles, California, Apr. 21–23, 1975). ACM Press, New York, NY, 105–113, 1975.

[30]. G. Kotonya, and I. Sommerville, “Requirements Engineering Processes and Techniques”, John Wiley & Sons, Chichester, UK, 2002.

[31]. B.W. Boehm, “Software Engineering Economics”. 1st. Prentice Hall PTR, 1981.

[32]. J.D. Procaccino, J.M. Verner, K.M. Shelfer, and D. Gefen, “What do Software Practitioners Really Think about Project Success”: an Exploratory Study. Journal of Systems and Software, 78, 2 (Nov. 2005), 194–203, 2005.

[33]. S.I. Anton, “Successful Software Projects Need Requirements Planning”, IEEE Software, 20, 3 (May–Jun. 2003), 44–47, 2003.

[34]. He Lulu, C. Carver Jeffrey, and B. Vaughn Rayford, “Using Inspections to Teach Requirements Validation”, January 2008.

[35]. Ian Sommerville, Gerald Kotonya. “Requirements Engineering”, ISBN: 0471972088. Authors. Publisher. John Wiley & Sons, 1998.

[36]. Gary E. Mogyorodi, “What is Requirements- Based Testing”, Author, Published in, March 2003.

[37]. B. BOEHM, “Industrial software metrics top ten list”, IEEE, 1987.

[38]. Donald Firesmith, ETH Zurich, “Common Requirements Problems”, Chair of Software Engineering ©JOT, Vol. 6. No.1, January-February 2007

[39]. Ian Sommerville, Pete Sawyer, “Requirements Engineering”, John Wiley & Sons, New York, 1997.

[40]. G. Buckberry, and J. Siddiqi, “Requirements Engineering”, Proceedings of first international conference on, IEEE, 1994, pp.230-238, 1994.

[41]. O. Laitenberger, T. Beil, T. Schwinn, "An industrial case study to examine a non-traditional inspection implementation for requirements specifications", Los Alamitos CA, 2002.

[42]. M. E. Fagan, "Design and Code Inspection to Reduce Errors in Program Development", IBM Systems Journal, vol. 15, 1976, pp. 182-211, 1976.

[43]. Oliver Laitenberger, “A Survey of Software Inspection Technologies”, Handbook on Software Engineering and Knowledge Engineering, Citeseer, 2002.

[44]. Steven R. Rakitin. “Software Verification and Validation for Practitioners and Managers”, Artech House Publishers, 2nd edition (August 1, 2001), 2001.

[45]. Tony Gorschek, Nina Dzamashvili – Fogelström, “Test-case Driven Inspection of Pre-project Requirements-Process Proposal and Industry Experience Report”, IEEE International Conference on Requirements Engineering, 2005.

[46]. Dr. E. Al-Qutaish Rafa, “Requirements Validation and Verification, “Requirements Engineering”, 2005.

[47]. J.C.S.P. Leite, P.A. Freeman, “Requirements validation through viewpoint resolution”, IEEE Transactions on Software Engineering, Vol. 17, 1991, pp.1253-1269m, 1991.

[48]. J. Fowler Floyd, “Survey Research Methods: Fundamental Principles of Clinical Reasoning & Research”, SAGE Publications, 2002.

[49]. Ian Sommerville, Pete Sawyer, Requirements Engineering, John Wiley & Sons, New York, 1997.

[50]. Tony Gorschek, Nina Dzamashvili – Fogelström, "Test-case Driven Inspection of Pre-project Requirements-Process Proposal and Industry Experience Report", IEEE International Conference on Requirements Engineering, 2005.

[51]. A.J. Albrecht and J.E. Gaffney, "Software Function and Development Effort Prediction: A Software Science Validation". IEEE Transaction on Software Engineering, (Nov. 2003), 639–648, 2003.

[52]. T. Olsson and P. Runeson, "A Feed-Back Approach to Validation of a GQM Study." IEEE Computer Society, 7th International Symposium on Software Metrics (Apr. 04–06, 2001). 236-242, 2001.

[53]. L.C. Briand, J. Wüst, J.W. Daly and V. Porter, "A Comprehensive Empirical Validation of Design Measures for Object-Oriented Systems". IEEE Computer Society, 5th International Symposium on Software Metrics (Mar. 1998), 246–257, 1988.

[54]. Y. Chen, B.W. Boehm, R. Madachy and R. Valerdi, "An Empirical Study of eServices Product UML Sizing Metrics". IEEE Computer Society, International Symposium on Empirical Software Engineering (Aug. 2004)., 199–206, 2004.

[55]. J. Robertson and S. Robertson, "Requirements Management: A Cinderella Story", Requirements Engineering Journal, (Sep. 2000), 134–136, 2000.

[56]. H. Sharp, A. Finkelstein, G. Galal, "Stakeholder Identification in the Requirements Engineering Process". In Proceedings of the Tenth

International Workshop on Database and Expert Systems Applications, IEEE, Los Alamitos CA, pp. 387-391, 2003.

[57]. B. Ramesh, M. Jarke, "Toward Reference Models for Requirements Traceability." IEEE, Transactions on Software Engineering (2001), 58-94, 2001.

[58]. N. Juristo, A.M. Moreno, A. Silva, "Is the European Industry Moving toward Solving Requirements Engineering Problems". IEEE, Software (2002), 19(6):70-78, 2002.

[59]. L.C. Briand, S. Morasca and V.R. Basili, "Defining and Validating Measures for Object-Based High-Level Design". IEEE Transaction on Software Engineering, (Sep. 1999), 722–743, 1999.

[60]. M.Y. Ivory, R.R. Sinha and M.A. Hearst, "Empirically Validated Web Page Design Metrics". In Proceedings of the SIGCHI Conference on Human Factors in Computing Systems (Washington). ACM Press, New York, 2001, 53–60, 2001.

[61]. V.B. Misic and D.N. Tesic, "Estimation of Effort and Complexity: an Object-Oriented Case Study". Journal of Systems and Software, (May 1998), 133–143, 1998.

[62]. P. Mohagheghi and R. Conradi, "An Empirical Study of Software Change: Origin, Acceptance Rate, and Functionality vs. Quality Attributes". In Proceedings of the2004 International Symposium on Empirical Software Engineering (Aug. 19–20, 2004). IEEE Computer Society, Washington, DC, 7–16. 2004.

[63]. G. Canfora, F. García, M. Piattini, F. Ruiz and C.A. Visaggio. "A Family of Experiments to Validate Metrics for Software Process Models". Journal of Systems and Software, (Aug. 2005), 113–129, 2005.

[64]. B. Bahli and S. Rivard, "A Validation of Measures Associated with the Risk Factors in Information Technology Outsourcing". In Proceedings of the 36th Annual Hawaii International Conference on System Sciences, (Jan. 06–09, 2003). IEEE, Computer Society, Washington DC, 269.1, 2003.

[65]. A. Preece, "Evaluating Verification and Validation Methods in Knowledge Engineering", University of Aberdeen, Computing Science Department, Aberdeen AB24 3UE, Scotland,2001,pp.l23-145, 2001.

[66]. P. Yu, T. Systa, and H.Muller, "Predicting Fault-Proneness Using OO Metrics: An Industrial Case Study". In Proceedings of the Sixth European Conference on Software Maintenance and Reengineering (Mar. 2002). IEEE Computer Society, Washington DC, 99, 2002.

[67]. T. Javed, M.E. Maqsood and Q.S Durrani, "A Study to Investigate the Impactof Requirements Instability on Software Defects". SIGSOFT Software Engineering Notes, 29, 3 (May 2004), 1–7, 2004.

[68]. M. Genero and M. Piattini, "Empirical Validation of Measures for Class Diagram structural Complexity through Controlled Experiments", 5th International ECOOP Workshop on Quantitative Approaches in Object-Oriented Software Engineering, Hungary (Jun. 2001), 2001.

[69]. M.C. Gaudel and G. Bernot, "The Role of Formal Specifications", IFIP State-of-the-Art Report: Algebraic Foundations of Systems Specification, 1999, Springer, 1999.

[70]. S.J. Andriole, "Fast cheap requirement prototype: or else". Drexel University, IEEE vol 11, mar 1994, pages 85-87, 1994.

[71]. Ian Graham, "Structured prototyping for requirements specification in expert systems and conventional IT project". IEEE vol 2, 1991, pages 82-89, 1991.

[72]. A. Davis, "Operational prototyping: A new development approach. Software", IEEE vol 9,issue 1992, pages: 70-78, 1992

[73]. St. Louis, "what is prototyping", university of Missouri, online document, 1997.

[74]. Hassan Ghoma, Douglas Scott: "prototyping as a tool in the specification of user requirements". IEEE vol 11, issue in 2005, pages: 333-342 , 2005

[75]. B.W. Boehm, "Software Engineering", IEEE Trans. Computers, Dec. 1976, pp. 1226-1241, 1976.

[76]. M. Lipow, B. B. Whit, and B. W. Boehm. "Software Quality Assurance: An Acquisition Guidebook", TRW-SS-77-07, November 1977 (IEEE Computer Society Repository No. R78-155), 1977.

[77]. B.W. Boehm, R. K. McClean, and D. B. Urfrig, "Some Experience with Automated Aids to the Design of Large-Scale Reliable Software", IEEE Trans. Software Engr., Mar. 1975, pp. 125-133, 1975.

[78]. T.E. Bell, D.C. Bixler, and M. E. Dyer, "An Extendable Approach to Computer Aided Software Requirements Engineering", IEEE Trans. Software Engr., Jan 1977, pp. 49-59, 1977.

[79]. M.W. Alford, "A Requirements Engineering Methodology for Real-Time Processing Requirements". IEEE Trans. Software Engr., Jan. 1977, pp. 60-68, 1977.

[80]. R.L. London, "A View of Program Verification". Proceedings, 2004 IEEE/ACM International Conference on Reliable Software, 2004.

[81]. Tira Cohene and Steve Easterbrook, "Contextual Risk Analysis for Interview Design", Proceedings of the 2005 13th IEEE International Conference on Requirements Engineering, 2005.

[82]. D. Nelsen, "System Engineering and Requirement Allocation", IEEE System and Software Requirements Engineering, IEEE Software Computer Society Press Tutorial, IEEE Software Society Press Los Alamos, California, 1990.

[83]. John W. Creswell, "Research Design Qualitative, Quantitative and mixed Methods Approaches 2nd Edition", SAGE Publications Inc, USA, 2003

[84]. M.G. Christel, D.P. Wood, and S.P. Stevens, "AMORE: The Advanced Multimedia Organizer for Requirements Elicitation", 1999.

[85]. R. Budde, H. Zullighoven, N. R. German, "proptotping revisted", CompEuro '90. Proceedings ofthe 1990 IEEE International Conference on Computer Systems and Software Engineering, IEEE Computer Society ,May 1990, ppAI8-427, 1990.

[86]. P. Locucopoulos and V. Karakostas, “System Requirements Engineering”, McGraw-Hill Book Company Europe,Berkshire,UK, 2005.

[87]. Summerville, “software Engineering”, sixth Edition, Indian reprints 2004.

[88]. V. Lalioti and P. Loucopoulos, "Visualisation for Validation", Fifth Conference an Advanced Information Systems Engineering, CAiSE, Springer-Verlag London, UK,June 1993, pp. 143 – 164, 1993.

[89]. U. Sebast, R.Chatley, I. Kramer, I.Magee, "Fluent-Based Web Animation: Exploring Goals for Requirements Validation", Proceeding of the12th IEEE International Conference on Requirements Engineering, IEEE Computer Society, September 2004, pp.208-217, 2004.

[90]. W. Vishnuvajjala, R.D. Zhang, "Use Case Maps for the Capture and Validation of Distributed Systems Requirements", IEEE Computer Society, Dept. of Computer. Sci., Minnesota Univ., Minneapolis, MN, 1999, pp.44, 1999.

[91]. D.R. Wallace, R.U. Fujii, "Software Verification and Validation: An Overview", IEEE Software, Vol 6 , Issue 3 IEEE Computer Society Press Los Alamitos, CA, USA, May 1989,pp. 10 -17, 1989.

[92]. F. Fabbrini, M. Fusani, S. Gnesi and G.Lami, “An automatic Quality for natural language requirement”. Seventh international workshop on requirement engineering: Foundation for software quality 2001.

[93]. F. Chantree.B. Nuseibeh, A.N. Roeck and A. Willis, "Identifying Nocuous Ambiguities in Natural Language Requirements", Proceeding of 14th IEEE International Conference on Requirements Engineerin, IEEE Computer Society"pp. 56-65, 1998.

[94]. V. Ambriola, V. Gervasi, "Processing natural language requirements", ASE, 12th IEEE International Conference on Automated Software Engineering (ASE'97) (formerly: KBSE), 1997, p. 36-37, 1997.

[95]. H.B. Reubenstein, & R.C. Waters, "The Requirements Apprentice: Automated Assistance for Requirements Acquisition". IEEE Trans. On Software Engineering, Vol. 17, No. 3, pp. 226-240, 1991.

[96]. A. F Ackerman, L.S. Buchwald, and F.H. Lewsky, "Software Inspections: An Effective Verification Process", IEEE Software, vol 6, no. 3, pp. 31-36, 2005.

[97]. R. Warhurst, and D. Flynn, "Validation JSD specifications by executing them", Information and software technology. 32 no. 9 November 1990.

[98]. C. Potts, "Determining Requirements for Evolving Systems", Tutorial Notes and Slides, CAiSE '97, Barcelona, Spain, June 1997.

[99]. D. Pandey, U. Suman, A. K. Ramani, "Design and Development of Requirements Specification Documents for Making Quality Software Products", National Conference on ICIS, D.P. Vipra College, Bilaspur, 2009.

[100]. S. Lauesen, "Software Requirements: Styles and Techniques", Addison-Wesley, 2002.

[101]. Dhirendra Pandey, Mohd. Waris Khan, Vandana Pandey "Role of Requirement Validation in Requirement Development", Proc. of International Conference on Recent Development in Engineering and Technology, Mysore, ISBN: 978-93-82208-29-7, pp. 97-101, 2012.

[102]. A. Terry, I. Bahill and J. Henderson Steven, "Requirements Development, Verification, and Validation Exhibited in Famous Failures", Wiley Inter Science, Systems Engineering, Vol. 8, No. 1, 2005.

[103]. D. Zowghi and N. Nurmuliani, "A study of the Impact of Requirements Volatility on Software Project Performance", Proc. of the Asia-Pacific Software Engineering Conference, UK, pp.3-11, 2007.

[104]. C. Urquhart, "Themes in Early Requirements Gathering: The Case of the Analyst, The Users and the Student Assistance Scheme. Journal of Information Technology and People, Vol. 12, No. 1, pp.44-54, 2009.

[105]. Kauppinen Marjo, Vartiainen Matti, Kontio Jyrki, Kujala Sari, and Sulonen Reijo, Implementing Requirements Engineering Processes throughout Organizations: Success Factors and Challenges, 2004.

[106]. Mantere Timo and T. Alander Jarmo, Evolutionary Software Engineering, 2005.

[107]. W. Foddy, Constructing Questions for Interviews and Questionnaires, Cambridge University Press, Cambridge, 1994.

[108]. Zowghi Didar and Coulin Chad, Requirements Elicitation: A Survey of Techniques, Approaches, and Tools, Cambridge University Press, 2005.

[109]. Kaufmann Morgan, Understanding Your Users: A Practical Guide to User Requirements Methods, Tools, and Techniques, Cambridge University Press, 2005.

[110]. Stetar Bill, "RE-tool your Workers", Journal of Advance Computer Manufacturing, Vol 5. No. 3, pp.77-97, 2000.

[111]. A. F. Osborn, Applied imagination, Charles Scribner's Sons, New York, 1999.

[112]. Ashish Chaudhary, Anil Punia, and Malhar Pujar, Requirements Engineering Role in Agile Development, John Willey Press, 2008.

[113]. E. Gottes, Requirements by collaboration. Addison Wesley, Boston, MA, 2002.

[114]. J. Nielsen, Clemmensen T, and C. Yssing, "Getting Access to what goes on in people's heads: Reflections on the think-aloud technique", Proc. of the 2nd Nordic Conference on Human-Computer Interaction, Aarhus, Denmark, pp.91-107, 2002.

[115]. J. A. Goguen JA and C. Linde, "Techniques for Requirements Elicitation", Proc. of the IEEE International Symposium on Requirements Engineering, San Diego, CA, pp.55-67, 2003.

[116]. E. Burge, et.al, "Software Engineering Using Rationale", The Journal of Systems and Software, Vol. 16, No. 3, pp.125-140, 2008.

[117]. A. Davis, et.al, "Effectiveness of Requirements Elicitation Techniques: Empirical results derived from a Systematic Review, 14th IEEE International Requirements Engineering Conference, Germany, pp.154-161, 2006.

[118]. C. J. Davis, et.al, "Communication Challenges in Requirements Elicitation and the use of the Repertory Grid Technique", Journal of Computer Information Systems, Vol. 5, No.2, pp.78-87, 2009.

[119]. D. Walz, J. Elam, and B. Curtis, "Inside a Software Design Team: Knowledge Acquisition, Sharing, and Integration", ACM Communications, Vol. 36, No. 10, pp.63-77, 2003.

[120]. B. Curtis, "Empirical Studies of the Software Design Process", Human-Computer Interaction- INTERACT '2000, Elsevier Science Publishers, North-Holland, pp.35-40, 2000.

[121]. O. Gotel, et al., "An Analysis of the Requirements Traceability Problem", Proc. of the IEEE International Conference on Requirements Engineering, Colorado Springs, pp.94-101, 2001.

[122]. B. Shneiderman, "Control Flow and Data Flow Structures Documentation: Two Experiments", Technical Notes: Human Aspects of Computing, Communications of the ACM Vol. 25, No. 1, pp.55-63, 2001.

[123]. S. B. Sheppard, E. Kruesi, and B. Curtis, "The Effect of Symbology and Spatial Arrangement on the Comprehension of Software Specifications", Proc. of 5$^{th}$ International Conference on Software Engineering, San Diego, CA, pp.207-214, 2001.

[124]. Ganska, et al, "Requirements Engineering and Design", Technology Report, Software Technology Support Center, Hill Air Force Base, 1995.

[125]. Gause, et al, Exploring Requirements Quality before Design, Dorset House Publishing, NY, 2009.

[126]. Kitchenham, Barbara, Pfleeger, and Shari Lawrence, "Software Quality: The Exclusive Target", IEEE Software, Vol. 13, No. 1, pp.12-21, 2006.

[127]. G. Ropohl, "Philosophy of Socio-technical Systems", In Society for Philosophy and Technology, pp.59-71, 1999.

[128]. Dhirendra Pandey, Ugrasen Suman, and A. K. Ramani, "Social-Organizational Participation difficulties in Requirement Engineering Process- A Study", Software Engineering Journal, BioInfo Publication, Volume 1, Issue 1, Mumbai, pp.01-05, 2010.

[129]. N. Juristo, A. M. Moreno, and A. Silva, "Is the European Industry Moving Toward Solving Requirements Engineering Problems?", IEEE Software, pp.70-77, 2002.

[130]. S. Komi-Sirvio and M. Tihinen, "Great Challenges and Opportunities of Distributed Software Development - An Industrial Survey", Fifteenth International Conference on Software Engineering and Knowledge Engineering, SEKE2003, San Francisco, pp.1-3, 2003.

[131]. R. Stevens, P. Brook, K. Jackson, and S. Arnold, Systems Engineering - Coping with Complexity, Prentice Hall, London, 1998.

[132]. J. D. Sailor, System Engineering: An Introduction. IEEE System and Software Requirements Engineering, IEEE Software Computer Society Press Tutorial. IEEE Software Society Press, 2000.

[133]. R. H. Thayer and W. W. Royce, Software Systems Engineering, IEEE System and Software Requirements Engineering. IEEE Software Computer Society Press Tutorial. IEEE Software Society Press. Los Alamos, California, 2000.

[134]. W. W. Royce, "Managing the Development of Large Software Systems", Proc. of IEEE Wescon, Reprinted in Proceedings 9th International

Conference Software Engineering IEEE Computer Society Press, Los Alamitos. California. USA, pp.328-338, 2007.

[135]. J. Siddiqi, "Requirement Engineering: The Emerging Wisdom", IEEE Software, pp.15-19, 1996.